ART AND LITERATURE IN
FOURTH CENTURY ATHENS

Art and Literature in Fourth Century Athens

by

T. B. L. WEBSTER

UNIVERSITY OF LONDON
THE ATHLONE PRESS
1956

Published by
THE ATHLONE PRESS
UNIVERSITY OF LONDON
at 2 Gower Street, London, w.c.1

Distributed by Constable & Co. Ltd.
12 Orange Street, London, w.c.2

U.S.A.
John de Graff Inc.
64 West 23rd Street,
New York, 10

Printed in Great Britain by
WESTERN PRINTING SERVICES LTD
BRISTOL

To
E. S. B.

To
L. S. B.

ACKNOWLEDGMENTS

I am grateful to the Hellenic Society for having given me the opportunity of delivering three Presidential addresses on Art and Literature in the fourth century B.C., which have grown into this book. The authorities of the Altes Museum, Berlin, the Fine Arts Museum, Boston, the City Art Gallery, Birmingham, the Ny Carlsberg Glyptotek, Copenhagen, the Hermitage Museum, Leningrad, the American School of Classical Studies in Athens, the Metropolitan Museum, New York, the British Museum and the Warburg Institute, London, and Lady Beazley have sent me the photographs for my illustrations; to all these I am deeply obliged. My wife and Mr. D. J. Furley read my first draft and Professor R. P. Winnington Ingram the second draft, and I have profited much from their help. Mrs. D. J. Furley helped me with the proofs and the index, and my wife read the page proofs. The staff of the Athlone Press have saved me from many blemishes. I offer them all my most sincere thanks.

14 *March* 1954   T.B.L.W.

TABLE OF CONTENTS

LIST OF PLATES

CHRONOLOGICAL TABLE

(Authors, artists, and works cited in the text)

Before 400   Isocrates b. 436. Plato b. 427.

        Prodicus, *Horae*. Timotheus, *Persae*. Lysias XII.

        Sculpture of Nike balustrade. Parrhasius painting. Pauson painting. Zeuxis painting.

        Attic vases by Nikias painter (Pl. 5*a*), Meidias painter (Pl. 7), Kadmos painter (Pl. 4*b*, 5*b*), Suessula painter, Pronomos painter, etc. (Pl. 2)—Group R and polychrome lekythoi.

400–390   Socrates d. 399.

        Plato's earliest dialogues. Philoxenus writing. Dicaeogenes, Spintharus writing tragedy; Meletus, *Oedipodeia*. Strattis, Demetrius writing comedy; Theopompus, *Mede*.

    398   Lysias XIII.

    395   Lysias XIV, VII.

    393   Lysias III. Theopompus, *Eirene*.

    391   Isocrates XI, XIII. Aristophanes, *Ecclesiazusae*. Plato, *Phaon*.

        Demetrius of Alopece working. Pastoret head, Actor relief, Stele of Ktesileos.

        Attic vases: Jena fragments, Meidias painter, Pronomos painter (Pl. 3*b*), Kadmos painter. Early South Italian red-figure vases.

390–380   Philoxenus d. 380. Aristotle, Demosthenes b. 384.

        Plato's early dialogues. Xenophon, *Anabasis, Memorabilia*. Antiphon (tragic poet) writing.

    388   Aristophanes, *Plutus*.

    387   Aristophanes, *Cocalus*. Foundation of Plato's Academy.

    386   First regular production of an old tragedy at the City Dionysia.

    380   Isocrates IV.

        Temple of Asclepius at Epidaurus. Early portrait of Socrates. Lyme Park relief (Pl. 1).

        Pamphilus painting.

        Attic vases: Kadmos painter, Meleager painter, etc. Early South Italian vases.

380–70 Plato: early to middle dialogues. Carcinus writing. *Rhesus* (?).

373 Theopompus, *Eirene*.

372 First tragic victory of Astydamas.

370 Isocrates x.

Praxiteles working (Pl. 6).

Attic vases. Early Apulian, Lucanian, Paestan vases.

373 Eirene of Cephisodotus.

370–60 Plato: middle to later dialogues. First tragic victories of Theodectes, Aphareus. Carcinus writing.

Ephippus, *Geryones*, *Nauagos*. Epicrates 11K.

367 Dionysius I victorious at the Lenaea. Aristotle joins the
Academy. Plato's second visit to Sicily.

360 Isocrates vii.

Praxiteles, Lysippus working.

Pamphilus, Euphranor painting.

Attic vases: early Kertch (Pl. 4a, 11). Early Apulian, Lucanian,
Paestan vases.

364 Praxiteles, Euphranor *floruerunt*.

360–50 Plato's latest dialogues, including *Phaedrus*. Aristotle, *Grylus*,
Protrepticus, *Eudemus*, *On Poets* (?). Cephisodorus, *Against
Aristotle*. Xenophon, *Hellenica* (?). Astydamas, Theodectes,
Chaeremon writing.

359 Isocrates, *Ep.* vi.

355 Isocrates viii, Demosthenes xx.

353 Isocrates xv. Theodectes, Theopompus *floruerunt*.

Praxiteles, Leochares, Scopas working.

Bronze hydria handle: Eros and Psyche (Pl. 13a). Actor terracottas.

Attic vases: early and middle Kertch painters (Pl. 10).

Early Apulian, Lucanian vases, Asteas group of Paestan.

353 Beginning of work on Mausoleum.

350–40 Plato d. 347. Menander, Epicurus b. 342.

Aristotle, *On Philosophy*: earliest version of *Rhetoric*, *Metaphysics*, *Ethics*.

Antiphanes, *Poiesis*. Eubulus, *Stephanopolides*.

349 Demosthenes i.

347 Demosthenes xx. Aristotle, elegiacs on friendship. Speusippus
at the Academy.

346 Isocrates v.

345 Aeschines I.

343 Demosthenes XIX, Aeschines II.

342 Aristotle, *Hymn to Virtue.*

341 Astydamas, *Achilles, Athamas, Antigone.* Euaretus, *Teucer,*
     Achilles. Aphareus, *Peliades, Orestes, Auge.*

340 Timocles, *Lycurgus.* Astydamas, *Parthenopaeus, Lycaon.*

     Tholos at Epidaurus. Tegea sculptures.

     Praxiteles, Scopas working.

     Stele of Prokleides. Copenhagen relief (Pl. 15). Bronze mirror
        in Berlin (Pl. 13*b*).

     Pausias and Nicias painting.

     Attic vases: middle and ripe Kertch painters (Pl. 16).

     Campanian, Paestan, Apulian, Lucanian vases. Early Gnathia
        vases (Pl. 3*a*).

340–30 Isocrates d. 338.

     Aristotle, *Poetics, Rhetoric, Ethics* (later versions).

     Alexis, *Agonis.* Timocles, *Heroes.* Originals of *Menaechmi,*
        Persa.

339 Isocrates XII. Xenocrates succeeds Speusippus at the Academy.

     First regular revival of an old comedy at City Dionysia.

334 Aristotle at the Lyceum.

330 Lycurgus, *Against Leocrates.* Aeschines III, Demosthenes XVIII.

     Rebuilding of the theatre and portraits of the tragic poets.
        Portraits of Aeschines, Alexander, later Socrates. Demeter of
        Cnidus. Stele from Ilissus. Stele of Axelos.

     Melanthius painting.

     Attic vases: ripe Kertch painters.

     Campanian, Paestan, Apulian, Lucanian, Gnathia vases.

340–39 Aixone relief.

336 Relief of Democracy and Demos (Pl. 8).

332 Apelles, Nicias *floruerunt.*

330–20 Aristotle, Demosthenes d. 322.

     Aristotle, later works including *Constitution of Athens.* ?Aris-
        toxenus, *Lives.* Philemon, *Emporos.* Diphilus, *Kleroumenoi.*
        Original of *Amphitruo.*

329 Timocles, *Ikarioi.*

328 Crates *floruit.*

324 [Demosthenes] XXV, Satyr-play, *Agen.*

321　Menander, *Orge*.

Lysippus, Leochares working. Portraits of Euripides (seated), Aristotle (Pl. 14), Alexander (bronzes), bronze boxer at Olympia. Lateran Poseidon. Ladies from Herculaneum.

Apelles painting. Aetion, *Alexander and Rhoxane*. Original of Alexander mosaic (Pl. 12), mosaic of philosophers.

Attic vases: ripe Kertch painters. Campanian, Paestan, Apulian (Pl. 9), Lucanian, Gnathia vases.

328　Lysippus, Silanion *floruerunt*.

320–10　Theophrastus, *Characters*. Menander, *Methe, Samia, Apistos, Synaristosai, Perikeiromene, Kolax*. Philemon, *Phasma*.

314　Zeno comes to Athens.

Tanagra figures.

Apelles painting.

Attic vases: late Kertch.

310–300　Demetrius of Phalerum writing. Original of *Rudens* (Diphilus).

306　Epicurus opens a school at Athens.

301　Zeno founds Stoic school.

Cephisodotus II working. Portrait of Demetrius Poliorcetes, Theophrastus.

Protogenes and Apelles painting.

After 300　Menander d. 292. Philemon d. 262.

Duris writing, Xenocrates (art historian) writing.

Philicus, Sositheus, Lycophron, Moschion writing: Gyges fragment (?).

Menander, *Second Adelphoi, Epitrepontes*. Philemon, *Panegyris, Thesaurus*. Apollodorus of Carystus writing.

Portraits of Demosthenes, Zeno, Menander, Epicurus.

Originals of portraits of tragic actor and poet. Pictures of New Comedy.

I

Introduction

I HAVE called this book *Art and Literature in Fourth-century Athens* for the sake of brevity, and I must here define each term in this title. Athenian seemed to me a better local description than Greek, because Athens was the intellectual capital of the Greek world and the three great philosophers, Plato, Aristotle, and Theophrastus, worked for most of their lives in Athens. I assume however (and shall try incidentally in the course of the narrative to justify the assumption) that communications in the Greek world were good and cross-influences many, and therefore I have not hesitated to quote works of art and literature produced in the rest of the Greek world where they have provided the best illustrations for my theme, but their connection with Athens is, I think, always clear.

Fourth-century is also not to be taken too literally. It would have been folly to exclude from my first chapter works of art or literature which formed a relevant part of the Athens in which Plato grew up, and in many cases dating is not so precise that we can say firmly that this must be between 410 and 400 and that between 400 and 390; but apart from the fact that no clear boundary divides the fourth century from the fifth, a knowledge of the late fifth-century background is so necessary for the understanding of early Plato that my procedure needs no apology. At the other end of the century I have been concerned above all to show New Comedy as a final flowering of Greek dramatic genius and I have not hesitated to include as many works of the third century

B

as I needed, but new developments such as Alexandrian poetry, Epicureanism, and Stoicism, however important they may be for the future, do not concern me and I have said as little about precursors of the Graeco-Roman period as I have of classical survivals in the late fifth and early fourth century.

It is more important still to define what I mean by Art and Literature. Many excellent works have been written on separate aspects of fourth-century Greece such as its history, its political ideas, its philosophy, its eloquence, its sculpture, its painting and its vase-painting. To these and to many other much more specialist studies I have been deeply indebted (and far more indebted than my references, which have been kept as brief as possible, will show). My purpose is to put in the centre what is for them rightly on the fringes and to extrude to the fringes or to banish altogether what is equally rightly the centre of their specialist studies. Central for me is the interrelation of thinkers, writers, and artists rather than their activity in their special field. I am not concerned with Plato as a metaphysician but as a critic of art and literature, as a writer of a particular kind of prose drama, and as manifestly open to influences from the art and literature prevalent in his youth and manhood. Nor am I concerned with Demosthenes as a patriotic politician or successful advocate but as a writer whose portraits can be compared with contemporary portraits in comedy and in art and whose prose can be brought into relation with the theories of prose style found in Aristotle's *Rhetoric*. Similar reasons have led me to say little of the minor orators and philosophers and little of Xenophon, nothing of architecture or coins, and not very much of the technical side of sculpture and painting.

For this limited purpose the material is adequate. There is plenty of prose, although we sorely miss Aristotle's dialogues and the literary criticism of Theophrastus; but sufficient fragments remain to form some idea of them. The loss of fourth-century tragedy is serious, but again the outlines can be drawn with the help of papyrus fragments, quotations, and the judgments in Aristotle's *Poetics*. We are considerably richer in comedy because we have the last two plays of Aristophanes at the beginning of the period and Roman adaptations of New Comedy (as well as copious papyrus fragments) at the end. For art the position is much the same as in the fifth century. We have some great architectural sculptures—e.g. the temples at Epidaurus and Tegea and the Mausoleum—and the long series of Attic grave-reliefs and documentary reliefs, a few original free sculptures, and many Roman copies; these last can be used with caution when they can be controlled either by their likeness to some known original or because they illustrate descriptions in ancient authors. We have a few trustworthy copies of great paintings, but again literary texts provide us with a history of painting in the fourth century and this history, in so far as it is a history of drawing, can be illustrated from the best Attic and South Italian vases and from the very fine engraved mirror-covers which were produced in Corinth and elsewhere.

The three philosophers dominate the fourth century rather as the three tragedians dominate the fifth century and I have accordingly named my three chapters after them. It seemed, however, impracticable to disentangle late Plato from early Aristotle or Aristotle from early Theophrastus. I have therefore ended my first chapter with Aristotle's arrival in Athens and my second with Aristotle's death. This division has other advantages: the great change in the style of painting (known to us best as the change from the rich style to the Kertch style in Attic red-figure vase-painting) and the beginning of the new rhetorical tragedy antedates Aristotle's arrival in Athens by only a few years, and Menander produced his first comedy the year after Aristotle's death, while Theophrastus' *Characters* can be dated only a year or two later. These divisions therefore correspond with major changes in art and literature.

The three philosophers, besides being thinkers adventuring in the realm of pure thought, were also critics of literature and art. One question which we shall have to consider is the relation between their criticism and contemporary practice: how far can their criticism be illustrated from contemporary practice, how far did it affect contemporary practice, and how did it respond to changes in contemporary practice? If there is a general truth in saying that Plato's ethical condemnation of literature and art changes with Aristotle and Theophrastus into aesthetic appreciation and scholarship, does this change correspond to a change in literary and artistic practice as well as to a change in the philosopher's outlook on the external world?

Besides these questions we have also to consider two other problems: how far were the philosophers in general affected by contemporary literature and art, and how far can parallels be drawn between their style and the style of contemporary literature and art. Theophrastus formulated clearly the distinction between language related to the audience, which was the language of the poet and rhetorician, and language related to the events, which was the language of the philosopher; his workmanlike prose belongs to the latter class and needs little description. Plato and Aristotle on the other hand were concerned with their audiences. Behind the treatises of Aristotle we can often sense the lecture which he delivered and we know enough of his dialogues to see something of their persuasiveness.

The dialogues of Plato and Aristotle are dramas of a particular kind and comparable not only to tragedy and comedy but also to carved or painted figures in a setting. Or we may increase the possible number of comparisons by thinking of the figures rather than the setting or the plot. Thus we can include in the same portrait gallery the characters of drama and philosophical dialogue, the character sketches drawn by the philosophers to illustrate their ethics, and the portraits drawn by orators, biographers, and historians, as well as the portraits executed by painters and sculptors. It may be objected that we are mixing real and imaginary portraits in the same gallery. Aristotle's great-souled man and Menander's Smikrines never existed and the sculptor of the Lateran Sophocles had never seen his original, but Demosthenes and Plato drew Aeschines and Socrates from the life, while

Silanion was a contemporary and fellow-citizen of Plato, whom he sculpted. But in fact this objection amounts to very little since the demand for historical verisimilitude in the modern sense was only in its infancy in the fourth century and Plato would no more have conceived of restricting Socrates' thought to the views which he actually held than a tragedian or sculptor would have conceived of representing Agamemnon as a Mycenaean warrior.

The common object of these portraits is to give a picture of another human being, to communicate to an audience certain opinions about him. What has often been called a development towards realism may equally well be called a change in the kind of opinions in which the audience is interested, and it is these changes which are primarily our subject. The communication of opinions about a person (alive, dead, or imaginary) is the common element in all portraiture. He is to be made intelligible, and being intelligible will awaken some reaction in the audience. The orator hopes that they will praise his client and blame his client's opponent. The historian may want to place his character in a favourable or unfavourable light. The dramatist designs the speeches of his characters to stir particular emotions in his audience. The carved or painted portrait is usually a lasting memorial of the virtues of its original. Even the philosopher's characterisations are seldom entirely neutral, since they occur in contexts which can roughly be labelled ethical. Thus, besides communicating information about his subject, the maker of a portrait usually selects his information to arouse a particular emotion in his audience.

Besides more detailed correspondences of style we shall notice three more general attitudes, which are in no way limited to portraiture. They are three different ways of treating material, not mutually exclusive and not confined to any one period but certainly more common each in its own period. In the early period it seems to me that artists and writers often look for contrasts in their material, contrasts such as god and man, reality and appearance, heroic and everyday life, and either express these directly or sometimes imply them by emphasising one term of the contrast.

In the middle period what is most interesting is the organic structure of statue, picture, drama, speech, or even sentence, and the composition is planned to have the maximum effect on the spectator or listener. In the last quarter of the fourth century the interest shifts from the structure to the surface and the details of external appearance, and the individual characteristics of the original are emphasised. I have called these ways of treating material or attitudes of mind and I shall give instances of them as I proceed. I believe that they are in fact attitudes of mind which were common in the early, middle, and late fourth century and that to appreciate them enables us to understand better the many disparate works of art and literature that survive. I have not used them as chapter headings or even as my first principle in grouping my material because, though such attitudes of mind may be characteristic of a generation, they are in no way confined to their generation but existed before it and survive after it. We are perhaps at the moment undergoing such a change of attitude ourselves, and have abandoned some of our belief in a succession of styles which made it possible to date absolutely any member of a series.

The interrelations of thinkers, writers, and artists can nowhere be more clearly perceived than in their use of personification. We shall meet personifications again and again in the course of this study, and it may be useful to discuss them very generally here. All through history Greek artists and writers might represent things, natural phenomena, and abstract ideas as living beings more or less anthropomorphic. It was a means of making abstract or formal material come alive, but also corresponded to a real element in primitive thought, an element which survives in much modern thought; any thing or idea which arouses strong emotion or is believed to be important is credited with some kind of life and power analogous to our own. In the fifth century the development of abstract and scientific thought gave rise to a very large number of new personifications to express the importance of the new ideas and as a kind of shorthand to explain them conveniently.

This is an important part of the fourth-century heritage, but the fourth century inherits also much that is much older. For instance the assumption of a world being, which goes back to Homer's Okeanos, can still be seen colouring Plato's Demiurge and even Aristotle's Physics. Here the personification is undoubtedly real and not ornamental. For the other personifications also, whether primarily explanatory like the personification of Tragedy in the *Poetics* or primarily persuasive like the personifications of Vices in Plato, we can perceive reasons why they are not mere ornaments but have some reality for their creators. Many of them have a history behind them, which was still a living history because pictures and statues survived, old plays were reproduced, epic was still recited. Sometimes the transition from the personification to the persons represented by it is easy, as when Hellas stands for the Greeks or Poetry stands for poets. Sometimes, as in the chariot of the Soul in Plato's *Phaedrus*, the action and scenery is taken over from a well-known story and therefore the soul is recognised as a new Heracles.

All such personifications are alive, but how lively they are depends on their author. We can usefully speak of deification, strong personification, and weak personification, as long as we remember that for literature these are not watertight compartments but points on a continuous scale and that the artist is restricted by his medium to full anthropomorphisation, though he can distinguish between persuasive personifications like the Furies with their whips and torches in the Hades scenes and ex-planatory personifications like Pompe (Procession) on an Attic jug (pl. 16). Deification (by which I mean the giving of a sacrifice or a hymn to a personification) corresponds presumably to some particular public need like that which caused the erection of Cephisodotus' Eirene and Plutus; private deification such as that of Philia as the mother of Zeus (pl. 15) is presumably rarer but also due to a particular need. Strong personification is either and more commonly the sign of the speaker's emotion (this is an idea which must be conveyed to the audience) or more rarely, as in

Aristotle's account of the growth of Tragedy, is caused by a trans-ference of terminology from another sphere, in that case biology. Weak personification includes the weaker persuasive personi-fications in the orators and other writers and what are often called hypostatised abstracts: the most interesting examples of these are perhaps the Platonic Ideas when they appear in argument and not fully personified as in the *Phaedrus* myth.

The tradition of personification is so strong that it is difficult to distinguish the peculiar characteristics of fourth-century personi-fication. It is probable that Chance (Tyche) and Opportunity (Kairos) (though not new) answered particular needs of the period. It is clear that Psyche, Eros, Methe (drunkenness), Agnoia (ignorance) and other personifications in art and literature are used to communicate the achievements of psychological and ethical analysis, just as the personification of the Arts corresponds to the growth of literary and artistic criticism and the renewed personification and deification of the stars results from increasing knowledge about their movements. The typical use in the orators is to fix an idea vividly in the minds of the audience, particularly in order to discredit an adversary, and it is far more common in the fourth than in the fifth century. In all these uses an idea comes alive and becomes a person, and this enlivening of the formal is one of the two basic tendencies of Greek art and literature.

The other tendency is to convert what is living or felt to be alive and powerful into a pattern which the mind can grasp. Seen the other way round, the deifications of abstract ideas may be instances of this, as the substitution of something more rational for the now old-fashioned Olympian gods. So also the assumption of a per-sonal divinity is grounded in late Plato in as much scientific physics and astronomy as he can find suitable for the purpose and in Aristotle the Demiurge becomes Nature, *physis*, which is much less personal in name than god and might become completely impersonal. More important still, the hierarchy of Platonic Ideas, sometimes fully personified and never less than hypostatised

abstracts, became for Aristotle a basis of biological classification
and a model for the gradation of logical universals in the syllogism. Thus both the two opposite tendencies, the enlivening of
the formal and the formalising of the living, continue to operate
in fourth-century literature and art.

II

Art and Literature in Plato's Athens

1. THE FESTIVAL CITY

ATHENS after the fall of the Thirty in 403 and during the early years of the Second Confederacy must have been on the whole a place of buoyancy and optimism. There was, it is true, great poverty after the Peloponnesian War, and the last two plays of Aristophanes show that it extended to the country as well as the town; it is true also that the comic poets (and therefore presumably a considerable or at least an influential part of their audiences) criticised the new forward policy, Conon's command of the Persian fleet and the formation of the Second Athenian Confederacy. But Athens had lost far less of her position through war, revolution, and counter-revolution than had seemed likely, and Isocrates' *Panegyricus*, in which he called upon Athens and Sparta to forget their jealousies and make common cause against Persia, is probably a fair statement of Athenian optimism in the eighties. One sentence expresses briefly the Athenian claim:[1] 'Our city has so far surpassed the rest of mankind in wisdom and its expression that her disciples have become the teachers of the world; the name of Greek no longer denotes a race but a kind of intellect, and men are called Greek rather because they share Athenian education than because of community of blood.' If this is true, what evidence can we see for an international Greek culture centred on Athens and what was its quality? Isocrates himself addressed rulers all over the Greek world. Plato had relations with Megara and Thebes, with Sicily and South Italy. The tragic poet

[1] Isocrates, iv, 50.

had to make his name in Athens before he could produce success-
fully in other Greek cities; we know that Dionysius of Syracuse
tried repeatedly to have his tragedies performed in Athens, and
the successful comic poet Antiphanes was apparently not an
Athenian citizen; moreover vases already show evidence of the
export of both tragedy and comedy to the Greek cities in South
Italy. The Sicyonian painter Pamphilus had painted in Athens
before 387, and the Athenian sculptor Cephisodotus worked in
Megalopolis and Thebes as well as Athens.[1]

In his summary of the benefits which Athens has given mankind Isocrates[2] first names agriculture and the Mysteries, then
speaks of Athens as a centre of colonisation, of the benefits of the
rule of law, and of the advantages of the Peiraeus as a central
market; he calls Athens a 'festival city', and finally personifies
Philosophy, 'who helped in the discovery and the execution of all
this, who educated us to action and made us kind to each other,
and distinguished between necessary evils and evils which arise
from our own folly'. It is not a bad picture of the Athenian spirit,
and the equation of humanity and discrimination with discovery
and execution is characteristic of Isocrates' time: Pericles in the
Funeral Speech had emphasised speed and brilliance more than
tolerance, but Isocrates is essentially developing the Periclean
ideal. He goes on to discuss eloquence as the distinctive mark of
this civilisation and here he is thinking particularly of his own
school. A practical school for politicians was a new idea and an
attempt to meet the political conditions of the time. It sounds to
us both unreal in so far as it was based on a superficial knowledge
of local history and too realistic in its concentration on the technique of speaking, but it was probably much better than anything
that had preceded it.

In his speech *Against the Sophists* Isocrates clearly distinguishes
his position both from those who profess instruction in political

[1] Ch. Picard, *Manuel d'archéologie grecque, la sculpture, III. Période classique
—IVe siècle* (hereafter quoted as Picard *IVe*), 15, discusses the travels of artists
and their teams in the fourth century.   [2] Isocrates, iv, 28–47.

eloquence, whom he charges with making their pupils learn model speeches by heart instead of exercising them, and from Plato. We should surely see a reference to Plato's discussions in the early dialogues of happiness, virtue, and temperance, when Isocrates attacks the professors of Eristic who 'are so bold that they try to persuade the young that if they come to them they will know what is to be done and this knowledge will make them happy'. Similarly, we may see an allusion to Plato's Ideal State in the Egyptian caste system described in the *Busiris* and a further allusion to the Socratic ethics of the early dialogues in the early part of the *Helen*. Nothing in these attacks goes beyond the reasonable rivalry of men who were competing for the same pupils and had fundamentally different ideas on the subject-matter of instruction. For Isocrates Plato was pretending to do something which could not be done; for Plato Isocrates was on the border-line between philosophy and politics and got the worst of both worlds.[1]

One permanent result however Isocrates did achieve. The conception of leisured educated prose discussing serious issues against a background of tradition originated with him. His style is a development of the style of Gorgias. Gorgias in the late fifth century had captivated his audiences by a highly artificial prose; its vocabulary was poetical and its clauses held together by parallelism of structure and antithesis. Isocrates loosened this up into what he called a 'flowery and gracious style'. He preserved the poetic flavour by avoiding hiatus and introducing frequent rhythmical elements particularly at the ends of paragraphs. While abandoning the extreme constriction of Gorgias' parallel and antithetic clauses, he preserves their structure as the basis of a larger fabric. Isocrates loves pairs of sentences, clauses, phrases, and words, connected by corresponsive particles, and this elaboration

---

[1] Isocrates, xiii, 9–13; 1–8; xi, 15; x, 1; Plato, *Euthydemus*, 305c. A recent sympathetic examination of Isocrates' claim to be an educator has been made by W. Steidle, *Hermes*, 80 (1952), 257. Isocrates on his own style: v, 27; xiii, 16; xv, 47; fr. 2.

by the paratactic construction of pairs rather than by the hypo-
tactic use of clauses and participial phrases gives his sentences an
entirely different structure from those of Lysias and Demosthenes.
The principle is simple: every sentence and clause is divided into
two antithetic halves, and each succeeding antithesis must depend
on or be subordinate to that immediately preceding it, so that the
result is a chain of small balanced parts, which may be of any
length. The other marked characteristic of his style is the padding
out of simple grammatical terms by the addition of synonyms or
near-synonyms. The style succeeds because the few rather simple
ideas of Isocrates are absorbed by the audience while they are
enjoying the construction of the chains of antithetic phrases.

   This style can reasonably be compared with the so-called rich
style of contemporary vase-painting and sculpture,[1] in which we
can trace the same kind of development as that which leads from
Gorgias to Isocrates. Obvious examples in sculpture are the balustrade of the temple of Athena Nike in Athens from the late fifth
century and the acroteria of the temple at Epidaurus from the
early fourth. The Victories of the Nike temple have their garments
arranged in an elaborate pattern of tiny folds; the drapery of the
Epidaurus figures is freer and less constricted but still the formal
pattern is dominant and clear. The colour has gone from these
sculptures, and we do not know how much it added to their rich-
ness; for that we must turn to vase-painting where we can see the
rich style in the Meidias painter, who started painting in the last
quarter of the fifth century, and in his successors, who continue
to the end of the first quarter of the fourth. The clothes in painting

   [1] For sculpture I give references, where possible, to the pictures in G. M. A.
Richter, *Sculpture and Sculptors of the Greeks*, as being probably the most acces-
sible collection. Nike balustrade: Richter, figs. 504–7. Epidaurus akroteria: figs.
710–12. Rich style in vase-painting, here, Pls. 3*b*, 4*b* and 5*b*, 7. For fourth-century
Attic vases the essential works are J. D. Beazley, *Attic Red-figure Vase-painting*
(quoted as *ARV* with page and no. of vase on page); K. Schefold, *Untersuchungen
ʒu den Kertscher Vasen* (quoted as Schefold, *U.*, with no. of vase in his catalogue);
H. Metzger, *Représentations dans la céramique attique du IVe siècle*, quoted as
Metzger with page and no. of vase on page).

too are immensely elaborate and their surfaces are either cut up into a multitude of tiny folds or covered with elaborate patterns. Moreover to the normal black of the background and red of the clay are added white for the flesh of women and Erotes and gold for their necklaces, bracelets, hair-ornaments, and other appurtenances.

In subject-matter as well as style Isocrates shows an affinity with contemporary art, since we can trace from the late fifth century a patriotic art which glorifies the past of Athens in the same spirit as the *Panegyricus*. Isocrates develops there a strain of thought which can be seen in some of the plays of Euripides, particularly *Suppliants*, *Erechtheus*, and *Ion*, and was probably the conception of Athens put forward by politicians like Theramenes, who believed in the 'ancestral polity'. Attic legends always figured on Attic vases[1] and there is nothing new in pictures of Erichthonius and Cecrops, of Theseus, or even of Triptolemus. It is however interesting that on the well-known hydria with the rape of the Leucippids in the British Museum[2] the Meidias painter adds to the Argonauts who accompany Heracles to the garden of the Hesperides the Attic tribal heroes Antiochus, Oineus, Akamas, Hippothon and Demophon. The expedition of the Argonauts has become a partly Athenian enterprise and a mythical ancestor for Attic colonisation (or, as we are accustomed to say, the Ionian migration), which Isocrates praises in the *Panegyricus*. On a pelike in New York[3] the same painter draws the poet Musaeus with Aphrodite and the Muses and by his side is Deiope with the

---

[1] Examples of Attic legends on vases of this period: *Erichthonius:* Palermo, *ARV*, 846/3. *Cecrops:* Cassel, *ARV*, 853/1. *Theseus:* Bologna, 303, *ARV*, 804/4, Pfuhl, *MuZ*, fig. 590. London, Armytage collection, *ARV*, 879, Metzger, 391/34. *Triptolemus:* Boston, 03.842, *ARV*, 834/2. Vatican, *ARV*, 882/41, Metzger, 240/1. On the treatment of the legend see Ch. Dugas, *Mélanges*, 1950, 20 f.

[2] E224. *ARV*, 831/1; Pfuhl, *MuZ*, fig. 593. For Attic tribal heroes in art of this time cf. Beazley, *AJA*, 39 (1935), 487; 54 (1950), 321; Van Hoorn, *Choes*, no. 83.

[3] New York, 37.11.23. *ARV*, 832/6; Metzger, 192/3; Richter, *AJA*, 43 (1939), 2. On the possible connection with Plato, *Rep.* 363c, see M. P. Nilsson, *Geschichte der griechischen Religion*, i, 651, 802.

infant Eumolpus. Deiope is an Attic heroine and Eumolpus figures constantly in pictures of the Eleusinian gods. Musaeus is here brought into the Eleusinian genealogy and his marriage is blessed by Aphrodite and the Muses. Musaeus and his son according to Plato assured the just a life of eternal drunkenness and provided a Hell for the unjust. It may be that the idea of reward and punishment for moral as distinct from ritual purity and impurity was introduced into the Eleusinian Mysteries in the late fifth century, and this may be the significance of bringing Musaeus into relation with the Mysteries. Possibly therefore we have in this vase evidence for the introduction into the Mysteries of a new strain of thought; certainly the association of Musaeus and the Muses with Eumolpus is a glorification of the Mysteries in the spirit of Isocrates.

The young knight Dexileos, who was killed in the war against Corinth in 394, had in his grave an oenochoe[1] with a picture of the statues of the Tyrant-slayers, and we know several similar representations on vases of the late fifth and early fourth centuries. Athens at this time consciously recalled the great second founding of the democracy, which produced the heroes of the Persian War. The watchword of the new democracy was *homonoia*, which meant primarily the agreement between the aristocrats and the democrats within the Athenian state (and was thus the ancestor of Cicero's *concordia ordinum*), but Isocrates widened it to mean agreement between the Greek states themselves.[2] An obvious symbol of this external *homonoia* is Cephisodotus' statue of Eirene holding the infant Plutus, which is believed to have been erected in celebration of the abortive peace with the Spartans in 373,[3] an event also celebrated by the comic poet Theopompus in his *Peace*.

---

[1] Boston, 98.936; Hahland, *Vasen um Meidias*, pl. 6a; Van Hoorn, *Choes*, no. 373. Cf. K. Schefold, *Mus. Helv.* 1 (1944), 197; 2 (1945), 263.

[2] *Panegyricus*, 3.

[3] The date depends on a combination of Pliny's date (372–68) for Cephisodotus' *floruit* with the introduction of the cult of Eirene soon after 375 (Isocr. xv, 109). Cf. Nilsson, *Eranos*, 50 (1952), 37. Richter, fig. 659 f. Theopompus: 7K, 1D. Papyrus fragment, *PSI*, no. 143. Ar. *Eccl.* 202.

In the comedy we can assume that Eirene, the personification of the peace so desperately needed that the Athenians deified her by decreeing her yearly sacrifices, spoke the prologue; a papyrus fragment which describes the frock of a bride whose wedding gifts are not gold or emerald but wisdom and justice is written in the same spirit, although we cannot say that it comes from this play. So also in the *Ecclesiazusae* Aristophanes speaks of Salvation (*soteria*) showing her face for a moment during the Corinthian war.

This idea of *homonoia* is symbolised in art by the pictures joining together two gods who normally belong to different spheres.[1] Apollo and Dionysus had shared the temple at Delphi long before this time, but now they were represented together in art; Apollo greets Dionysus and his thiasos at Delphi, or is served with food and drink by satyrs and maenads while the young Dionysus looks on. On another vase the young Heracles is reconciled to Apollo with the approval of Hera and Artemis, and on yet another Dionysus holds a symposium with the young Hephaestus. The painters represent *homonoia* in heaven to symbolise the *homonoia* which is so much desired on earth.

2. PORTRAITURE

The rich style is common on early fourth-century grave-reliefs but occasionally they show another style which we shall find also in other kinds of portraits. I start with two which may be dated in the first quarter of the century. The first[2] is typical of the considerable number of surviving early fourth-century grave-reliefs in the rich style. A bearded man, Ktesileos, stands with clasped hands before a seated woman, Theano, who raises her cloak with

---

[1] *Apollo and Dionysus:* Leningrad, St. 1807; *ARV*, 804/5; Metzger, 177/32. London, B.M., F 77; *ARV*, 866/4; Metzger, 177/33; Pickard-Cambridge, *Dithyramb*, fig. 2. *Apollo and Heracles:* London, B.M., 1924.7–16.1; *ARV*, 867/6; Metzger, 176/30. *Dionysus and Hephaestus:* Al Mina; Beazley, *JHS*, 59 (1939), 30, no. 82; Metzger, 126/34. *Dionysus and Aphrodite* (cf. Plato, *Symp.* 177e): Barcelona; Metzger, 187/37. Cf. Metzger, 128 f., 168 f., 183 f., on these scenes.

[2] Athens, NM., 3472. Johansen, *Attic Grave Reliefs*, 40, fig. 21.

the bridal gesture to display her beauty. We cannot tell which of them it is whose death is commemorated. They are shown as they were in life, except that the husband's contemplation has an intensity which moves us extremely because we know that one of them is dead. They are not individualised. They are a man and a woman in the prime of life. So they were and so they would be remembered. The other, the Lyme Park relief,[1] which is unique among grave-reliefs of the period, shows both emotion and individualisation. It is the monument of a comic poet. He sits with a scroll in his left hand, a slave mask in his right, and an old man's mask on the wall behind. His beard is cut short, the brows and cheeks are deeply furrowed, and the mouth is turned down at the corners. The face is much more individual than the face of Ktesileos. It is so individual that it would be perfectly possible for a later artist to create a new portrait from it, and we have to reckon with the possibility of such ancestors for later portraits of important men, just as this sculptor seems also to have created the later popular type of seated poet holding mask and/or scroll. The face displays much more emotion than Ktesileos. The sculptor stressed the contrast between the gay immortality of the poet's creations and the sad and disillusioned mortality of their creator. This is a contrast of the same kind as that which Plato makes Alcibiades draw in the *Symposium* (215) when he contrasts the satyric appearance of Socrates with the divine words which he speaks, and I think we have to ask whether other realistic portraits may not imply, if they do not express, such a contrast.

The relief of Ktesileos and Theano carries on the tradition of the white lekythoi of the third quarter of the fifth century, which are so moving just because they express so little emotion. This suppression of emotion and of individuality is typical of early fourth-century grave-reliefs and need not be further illustrated. It was presumably also typical of early fourth-century portraits although I do not feel certain that we possess an example. The

[1] Here, Pl. 1. Lyme Park, Stockport. Webster, *Studies presented to D. M. Robinson*, i, 590, pl. 55.

suggestion that the long-haired smiling strategos in Copenhagen, the Pastoret head,[1] is Conon, to whom the first public memorial statue was decreed, is certainly attractive. Such portraits are, as Isocrates says, 'a memorial to the virtues rather than to the bodily appearance' of their original.

The Lyme Park relief, although isolated among grave-reliefs, also has ancestors and contemporaries. Nearest in kind are the late fifth-century white lekythoi of Group R, especially the two which Professor Rumpf[2] has interpreted as illustrating the art of Parrhasius. 'If one reads the famous passage in Xenophon's *Memorabilia* (III, x, 1), it seems to be a contemporary's explanation of our two lekythoi. They do really represent τὸ τῆς ψυχῆς ἦθος and it is in fact μιμητὸν ἐν τοῖς ὄμμασιν. One is σκυθρωπός, the other φαιδρός; one μεγαλοπρεπής, the other φρόνιμος'. The comic poet on the Lyme Park relief is σκυθρωπός, and like the young man on the lekythos he shows it in the eyes; it is also shown in the narrow mouth with downward turned corners. Parrhasius was a painter; a contemporary painter was Pauson.[3] He according to Aristotle painted pictures of men worse than ourselves, which should not be shown to the young. He was a caricaturist, and we can imagine his art from an oenochoe[4] of the late fifth century, on which a smith with a turn-up nose, untidy hair and beard but elaborate embroidered chiton receives a tray of offerings from a little man with a bald head and very strange toes. Pauson seems also to have painted pictures of comedy (to which we shall return later). The realism in all these works is one term of a contrast: between the old, sad poet and his creations, between the young warriors and their promise, between the smith's festal robes and his face, and in the comedy pictures either between the characters and their heroic names, or between the grotesque appearance of

---

[1] Copenhagen, Ny Carlsberg, 438. Demosthenes, xx, 69. Isocrates, ii, 36.

[2] *AJA*, 55 (1951), 7.

[3] Texts in Overbeck, *Schriftquellen*, 1078–9, 1110 f. Particularly Aristotle, *Poet.* 1448 a 6, *Pol.* 1340 a 36. Aristophanes, *Ach.* 854, *Pl.*, 602.

[4] Here, Pl. 2. Athens, Agora Museum, Inv. P15210. Cf. Plato, *Rep.* 495e.

the characters and the normal appearance of the unmasked actors. Rather later, about 350 B.C., on a Tarentine fragment[1] showing a tragic actor coming forward to ask for applause, 'the painter', as Professor Rumpf has said, 'is fascinated by the contrast between the heroic mask of the fair curly-haired man and the elderly almost brutal face of the grizzled actor with his stubbly beard and his receding hair, which still shows the pressure of the mask'.

Is it justifiable to interpret sculptured portraits of the same kind in this same way? Demetrius of Alopece, whose active life seems to have extended from the late fifth century into the early fourth, made a portrait of the Corinthian general Pellichus, which is described by Lucian[2] as a figure 'with a prominent stomach, bald, his cloak falling off him, his beard blown into disarray, his veins clearly marked, the very image of the man'. That such realism in fact existed in sculpture of the late fifth and early fourth century is proved not only by the Lyme Park relief but by certain coins of Cyzicus with a wreathed head of repellent aspect and by the Farnese head[3] of Socrates, flat-faced, snub-nosed and bald, which should probably be combined with a standing body displaying his huge stomach. Plato's Alcibiades was alive to the contrast between Socrates' satyr-like appearance and his divine wisdom. The general may be interpreted in the spirit of Archilochus: it does not matter how ugly a general is if he is full of courage.

The elements in these portraits are realism, simplicity and contrast. This seems to me the same kind of art which we find in the two late plays of Aristophanes.[4] The reduction of the proportion of choral lyric to dialogue throws more emphasis on the characters. We have in Blepyrus, Chremes, and Pheidolus (if he is rightly so named) in the *Ecclesiazusae* and in Chremylus and Blepsidemus in the *Plutus* simple sketches of ordinary citizens of Athens. Chremes

[1] Here, Pl. 3*a*. Würzburg, 832. Rumpf, *JHS*, 67 (1947), 14; Webster, *JHS*, 71 (1951), 223, no. 37; *Greek Theatre Production*, no. A34.

[2] Lucian, *Philopseud.* 18.

[3] Cyzicus coins, Picard, *IVe*, 207 f. Farnese Socrates: Picard, *IVe*, 148; Richter, fig. 227 (Munich bronze).   [4] See my *Studies in Later Greek Comedy*, 22 f.

in the *Ecclesiazusae* is the loyal citizen who believes that it is his duty to carry out the Assembly's policy, although he has had no part in deciding it; he is contrasted with Pheidolus who first refuses to contribute to the common store because the Athenians may change their mind but hurries off to do it as soon as he hears that there is a free feast. In the *Plutus* Chremylus and Blepsidemus are similarly contrasted: Chremylus is the simple, generous man who has invited his friends to share his unexpected good fortune, while Blepsidemus is a realist who knows that wealth is not got without foul play. These characters with Blepyrus in the *Ecclesiazusae* and the wife in the *Plutus* (whom Murray describes as a 'nice, ignorant, pious Athenian *hausfrau'*) stand somewhere between the hags, lovers, sycophants and other stock characters, who appear in the later scenes of both plays and are in the tradition of fifth-century caricature, and the fantastic/heroic figures of Praxagora in the earlier and Penia (Poverty) in the later play, of which more will be said later. The simply drawn everyday characters are contrasted both with the streak of idealism, which can be apprehended behind the earlier scenes of both plays, and with the broad farce of the later scenes, which alone harmonise with the goggling masks and obscene costumes worn by all.

Another set of portraits roughly contemporary with these two plays are the generals in the second book of Xenophon's *Anabasis* (Ch. 6). The three sketches are balanced against each other and a little personal detail is added: the martinet Clearchus was fierce in face and harsh in voice; Proxenus, who graduated from Gorgias to Cyrus, was more afraid of the soldiers than they of him; the selfish and immoral Menon used the affections of other men for his own ends. These pictures are drawn in simple clear lines with nothing irrelevant—the bristling but effective general, the educated but ineffective general, and the complete realist. In the *Hellenica* Xenophon occasionally introduces personal incidents into his history, sometimes, as Bruns notes,[1] with an apology, since they fall

---

[1] *das literarische Porträt*, 36 f. Return of Alcibiades: Xenophon, *Hell.* I, iv, 13 f.; Duris ap. Plut., *Alc.* 32.

outside the range of his predecessor, Thucydides. Thus, when Alcibiades returns to Athens, 'as he sailed in, a crowd from the Peiraeus and from Athens collected to wait for the ships, wondering and wanting to see Alcibiades'; his friends praised and his enemies blamed his policy; 'when Alcibiades' ship anchored, he did not disembark at once because he feared his enemies. Then he saw his cousin Euryptolemus with his other relations and friends, and disembarked and went into the city in the middle of a band who were prepared to ward off any attack.' Alcibiades' arrival was also described some sixty years later by Duris of Samos. His picture is quite different: 'the oarsmen of Alcibiades rowed to the flute of the Pythian victor Chrysogonus; they kept time to the shouts of the tragic actor Callippides; both wore their festival robes. The ship sailed into the harbour under a purple sail.' Duris substituted for the simple and very effective realism of Xenophon a Hellenistic pageant.

The same kind of relevant realism can be found in the speeches of Lysias.[1] Anyone who knows the orator remembers him by the farewell scene in prison, the cripple's account of his riding, Simon's raid on a private house, or Euphiletus' account of the tricks used by his wife to conceal her lover. The speech against Eratosthenes is extremely interesting in this respect, if one imagines what Demosthenes or Aeschines would have made of it fifty years later. When he discusses Eratosthenes, Lysias says nothing of his opponent's private life but only speaks of his political actions at the two revolutionary periods, 411 and 403, which are relevant to the public inquiry then being held into Eratosthenes' conduct.[2] In describing the raid on his own house[3] Lysias is realistic because he wants to paint an unforgettable portrait of Eratosthenes, a portrait which should make all thought of an amnesty impossible. He starts with contrasting pictures of his own family and the Thirty: (a) 'we so lived under a democracy that we neither committed a crime against our fellows nor were

---

[1] Lysias, particularly 13, 39; 24, 10; 3, 5; 1, 6.
[2] 12, 42–61.
[3] 12, 4–23.

wronged by them,' (b) 'they thought it a small thing to take lives and a great thing to take money.' The exciting, staccato narrative of Lysias' arrest and escape is followed by the pathetic narrative of Polemarchus' death and burial, which leads up to a climax, contrasted portraits of Lysias' family and the Thirty, which repeat and develop the earlier contrast. The essential technique, contrasts and a limited but very effective realism, seems to be characteristic of portraiture in this period.

As a last example we may look at the series of portraits which Plato paints in the *Republic*[1] to show the stages between the philosopher and the tyrant. Plato's men make a series of four who decrease in reason and self-control and increase in passion, but he makes this series into a family tree and so provides not only a character sketch but an account of the upbringing which produces the character. The 'timocratic' man is the son of a good father, who lives in a bad city and therefore refuses every sort of office; the son, hearing his father criticised by his mother, the servants, and outsiders, embarks on an ambitious pursuit of political honour based on a military career. He is fond of the arts without much knowledge of them, cruel to slaves and more interested in money as he grows older. When he comes to disaster in the law-courts after holding some major command, his son turns to money-making, becomes thrifty and hard-working, is just in contracts for the wrong reasons, likes to be a guardian of an orphan because it gives a chance of injustice, and has no interest in education or in honours if they cost money. He is governed by the consuming passion of money-making. His son, brought up without education and thriftily, tastes 'the honey of the drones' and so pursues a course between the thriftiness of his father and complete abandonment to passion; he yields to each whim in turn, sometimes drunk, sometimes sober, sometimes taking exercise, sometimes idle, sometimes a philosopher, sometimes a politician, now with the war party, now with the moneyed party. His son, born when he

[1] *Rep.* 549d, 553, 559, 572. Cf. K. Vretska, *SO*, 30 (1953), 42 on these portraits and the contrasts between them.

is old, brought up in his easy-going law-abiding ways, is tempted further by passion. His only concern is feasts and *hetairai*, and so he falls into financial difficulties, borrows money, steals from his parents, becomes a robber and sycophant and finally a tyrant.

These sketches are brief and general but extremely vivid—the touches of home life, the references to careers, the mention of orphans and *hetairai* make them come alive. This is the summary art of Aristophanes or of early fourth-century painters and sculptors. Aristotle's sketches in the third and fourth books of the *Nicomachean Ethics* (to which we shall return later) lack this vividness, because he is more concerned with definition than portrayal and scarcely concerned at all with development. We have now to consider the earlier Platonic dialogues more generally as works of art. If we find there too threads which lead across to the art of the festival city, we shall have to define carefully the charges which Plato makes against art and literature in the *Republic*.

3. PLATO'S DIALOGUES

Philosophical dialogues are a particular kind of drama, a drama in which the plot is the movement of thought, the discovery of a truth or of the impossibility of discovering truth. In its purest form the speakers are merely holders of philosophical views and need have no other personality, but the earlier dialogues of Plato are dramatic in a further sense. They are concerned with particular occasions on which truth emerged from a combat between Socrates and various adversaries with clearly distinguished views, which may be presented at some length. The characterisation proceeds sometimes beyond their thought to their language, e.g. in the speech of Agathon in the *Symposium*. The personalities in the earlier dialogues stand out as memorably as the characters in a drama, not only Socrates and his immediate circle in the tragedy of his last days as we know it from the *Apology*, *Crito*, and *Phaedo*, not only the great sophists Protagoras, Hippias, Gorgias, Thrasymachus and the rest, but also others who have no place in the history of thought but nevertheless represent a particular viewpoint such as Euthyphro, Ion, Charmides, or Polemarchus. Their individuality appears most clearly in the opening scenes: thus in the *Charmides* Socrates returns from military service at Potidaea and visits the gymnasium of Taureas where he finds Chaerephon and Critias, then the beautiful young Charmides makes his entry. In the *Protagoras* Socrates explains how he had scarcely paid any attention to Alcibiades because he had met Protagoras, and then he describes how he was woken up early in the morning by a young man who wanted to hear Protagoras and then they made their way to the house where the sophist was staying. In the *Republic* the conversation grows in the house of Cephalus where Polemarchus had collected a party of friends who had come to the Peiraeus to see the festival of Artemis Bendis. The combat proceeds by set types of argument varied by interruptions—the intervention of Thrasymachus in the first book of the *Republic* and of Callicles in the *Gorgias*[1]—and in the longer dialogues the truth achieved, or something beyond what argument can achieve, is made clear by transposition to the plane of myth.

Each dialogue starts from a particular situation, a scene which stands vividly before our eyes with clearly distinguished characters even where the main dialogue is itself inserted in the framework of another dialogue as in the *Phaedo* and *Symposium*. Each dialogue has a single subject, and a broad distinction can be drawn between the dialogues in which an answer is achieved and the dialogues which achieve no answer. The latter class, which is numerically much larger, conforms to the description of modern education in the *Sophist*.[2] There the stranger describes a method of expelling the conceit of the expert: 'they question them about their expertise; then their opinions are easily shown to be unstable and self-contradictory'. This is a sufficient description both of the characters and of the procedure of the aporetic dialogues. They are primarily, as the stranger says in the *Sophist*, a purificatory

---

[1] *Rep.* 336b; *Gorgias*, 481b.
[2] *Soph.* 230, cf. V. Goldschmidt, *Les Dialogues*, 29 f.

exercise and do not arrive at a positive conclusion, partly because the experts divert the argument and prevent the possibility of a conclusion. But the conceited expert and the demonstration of self-contradiction are common enough also in the other dialogues. Because of their conceit the experts burst into the argument and so make it lively whether they divert it into a new direction or not. We have mentioned the intervention of Thrasymachus in the first book of the *Republic* and Callicles in the *Gorgias*; in the *Charmides*[1] Critias is angry with Charmides' answers, like a poet when an actor spoils his play. Or they may turn on Socrates and accuse him of acting like a torpedo fish or of leading the argument to a false conclusion by skilfully blocking his opponent's moves.[2]

Socrates himself comes out clearly by self-revelation and in the description of others not only as a ruthless thinker, whose homely illustrations are steps in arguments constructed like the arguments of mathematics,[3] but also as a person of great humour and of great courage in public and in private life, a person whose mother and wife are made known to us, of whose last thirty years we hear a good deal down to the death-scene of the *Phaedo*, a person finally of remarkable physical appearance. The contrast between the satyr outside and the god inside has already been mentioned in connection with the early sculptured portrait of Socrates. Plato had the double object of expounding his philosophy and of setting up a memorial to his teacher. In his own medium he had as models the memoirs of Ion of Chios and philosophical works analogous in form to the Melian dialogue. In fusing them into a new whole he preserved and exploited the contrast between Socrates as a person and Socrates as a thinker, just as on a smaller scale and in a different medium the sculptor of the Lyme Park relief commemorated a comic poet by preserving and exploiting the contrast between the sad, disillusioned old man and his gay creations.

This range from the bold abstract thinker to the lovable and very curious human being distinguishes Plato's Socrates from the

[1] *Charm.* 162d.   [2] *Meno*, 80; *Rep.* 487b.
[3] See most recently R. Robinson, *Plato's Earlier Dialectic*.

Socrates of Xenophon's *Memorabilia* and *Symposium*. The *Memorabilia* is a long series of mostly brief conversations with no setting (even the Euthydemus conversation has far less setting than any early Platonic dialogue), by which Xenophon seeks to demonstrate how useful Socrates was to his friends. Socrates is a shrewd, practical and spiritual adviser and nothing else. The Xenophon dialogues lack both the realism of Plato's character-drawing and the movement of thought which makes the plot.

Each early Platonic dialogue, as we have said, has a single subject and proceeds through various stages to an impasse or to a conclusion which may be transposed into the terms of a myth. The stages are marked sometimes by interventions and sometimes by imagery as when the argument is described as a journey or a hunt. They can be regarded as roughly parallel to the progression of thought described at the end of the sixth book of the *Republic* in the sense that there is always a progression from concrete cases to ideas and often an application of the idea achieved to everyday life. We can also see other principles of composition besides the forward movement to climax and conclusion; cross references and recurring imagery knit the whole together, and particularly in the *Euthydemus* the recurrent passages of eristic form a sort of pattern. Just as the portraiture may be compared to other portraiture, so also we shall find the imagery and the myths owe much to contemporary art. Nevertheless Plato expelled Drama and Illusionistic Art from the Ideal State.

4. PLATO'S CRITICISM

Plato's criticism of art and literature in the *Republic* is too well known to need quoting in detail. It is partial criticism based on three fundamental ideas: first, art and literature, whatever their practitioners may claim, do not and cannot give knowledge. Secondly, they display gods and heroes behaving in ways which the philosopher knows to be unworthy of their superior rank; and thirdly, art and poetry appeal so strongly to the irrational part of the soul (and this applies particularly to dramatic literature) that the spectator becomes like the unworthy subjects presented to his sight and hearing. Through this dramatic or illusionistic presentation the spectator is in immediate communication with the artist or poet: herein for Plato lies the danger of realistic art and dramatic literature, which like cosmetics and 'cuisine' only come into the ideal state when it has already grown feverish,[1] but herein also lies the possibility that an educational art could provide a 'healthy place' in which the young may develop into friendship and sympathy with fair reason. Most Athenians would have seen their festival city as such a healthy place, but reluctant refusal to admit tragic poets or illusionistic artists is the logical position for Plato to reach from his own first principles. The defence of poets and artists has been undertaken by many champions, and Plato's earlier contemporary Alcidamas[2] appreciated the realism and emotionalism which he despised; our present task is to describe the art and literature which Plato rejected and to ask whether we can see any kind of interaction between him and it.

We have already said a good deal about realism in art and it is reasonable to suppose that Plato would have preferred the grave-relief of Ktesileos to the Lyme Park relief. For him it would seem unworthy that a great poet (and the mere size of the relief shows that he was a man of some considerable importance) should be represented as old, sad, and disillusioned. By the same standard he would condemn the other realistic portraits that we have discussed, and Zeuxis' picture[3] of Menelaus bathed in tears at Agamemnon's tomb would seem to him as unworthy as Homer's Achilles rolling on the shore in lamentation for Patroclus. The expression of emotion by those who should not express emotion is one danger; the other is, quite simply, deception by illusionistic technique. Perspective and shading made it possible for the painter to convert a flat surface into something which was at any rate accepted as three-dimensional space. The development of

---

[1] *Rep.* 373b. [2] Cf. F. Solmsen, *Hermes*, 67 (1932), 133 f.
[3] Overbeck, 1677, Tzetzes, *Chil.* viii, 390.

perspective and shading in the late fifth and early fourth century can
be seen on contemporary vases (in spite of their limited range of
colours, on which much of the new technique depends) as well as
read in the ancient accounts of the art of Agatharchus, Apollo-
dorus, Zeuxis and others, to whom advances in perspective,
shading and highlights are attributed.[1] An interesting, though not
entirely successful, instance of this kind of painting is a fragment
of a krater in Jena:[2] Ariadne, Dionysus, and Eros are seated in
front of a temple. The temple is drawn in perspective and the
white of the exterior surfaces of columns and other architectural
members stands out from the contrasting red and black of the
underside of the roof beams. In the foreground, the white figures
of Ariadne and Eros tend to throw Dionysus back a little from the
front plane, while the temple recedes behind him. His thighs and
the cloak over his arm show considerable shading and therefore
solidity. Shading on clothes, bodies, and inanimate objects is combined with violent realism of emotion and action in the magnificent
Gigantomachies[3] of this period, in which not only is the eye
deceived by *skiagraphia* but the mind should be shocked by the
absence of divine calm.

We know something also about lyric poetry and tragedy in the
first thirty years of the fourth century. Timotheus' *Persae* seems
to have been produced at the very beginning of the period and
shows a curious mixture of style between the extreme realism of

[1] Cf. Rumpf, *JHS*, 67 (1947), 10 f.

[2] Jena, 382; Metzger, 144/75; Hahland, *op. cit.*, pl. 16a. Cf. also (*a*) Leningrad,
B2338, Schefold, *U.*, no. 239. Symposium with flute girl. In the far distance two
white columns, then couch with four banqueters (in red of ground except for
white cushion), then white flute girl, then in the foreground couch with two
banqueters (in red of ground but with long white rug). The depth is marked
partly by the overlapping of figures and objects, partly again by the alternation of
colours: white, red, white, red, white. (*b*) White lekythos, Berlin, F2685. Rumpf,
JHS, 67 (1947), 11; *Malerei und Zeichnung*, 122, pl. 39/4. Shading for garments,
and on the male figure close hatching, which follows the anatomical structure of
the body. Cf. also my article in *Symbolae Osloenses*, 29 (1952), 9 f.

[3] e.g. Naples, Inv. 2045. *ARV*, 850/3; Hahland, *op. cit.*, pl. 9, 10a. Paris,
Louvre, S.1677. *ARV*, 852/6. Pfuhl, *MuZ*, fig. 584. Cf. also the sculptured Sack
of Troy at Epidaurus, Richter, fig. 716/19.

the Asiatic's appeal for survival and the exotic ornamentation of overpressed metaphors. Even in the hands of a Milesian the historical Persian world of less than a hundred years before fades into a timeless unreality and an Eastern mist, such as are peculiarly apparent in contemporary pictures of Orientals, in which Sabazius, Cyrus, Thoas, Amazons, Arimaspians and Ethiopians wear the same clothes and are with difficulty distinguishable.[1] Philoxenus of Cythera was another lyric poet known in Athens in the first twenty years of the fourth century. In his *Cyclops* Polyphemus fell in love with the sea nymph Galatea, a curious crossing of two different mythological strains, for which there are parallels in the *homonoia* scenes of contemporary art.[2] Zeuxis' picture of the Centaur family, which is described at great length by Lucian, may also be mentioned as showing a similar interest in the private life of monsters. There are a few fifth-century pictures of satyr families but they are rare, and this humanisation of monsters is something new which looks forward to the Hellenistic age. In the fragments of Philoxenus the Cyclops serenades Galatea in conventional style, Odysseus asks what monster this is with whom he has been shut up, and the Cyclops tells him that he shall be sacrificed because he has sacrificed one of the Cyclops' sheep. The poem was much parodied in Athenian comedy and was probably given a political interpretation there as a satire against Dionysius of Syracuse. The other poem which should perhaps be ascribed to this famous Philoxenus (rather than to a little known Leucadian) is a long description of a feast in dithyrambic style (it is not irrelevant to remember Plato's strictures on Homeric descriptions of feasting and his equation of 'cuisine' and poetry as arts of

[1] *Sabazius*, London, British Museum, E695. Metzger, 148/79. *Cyrus*, Leningrad, St. 1790. *ARV*, 84/1. *Thoas*, Ferrara, T1145. *ARV*, 875; *Greek Theatre Production*, no. A8; Metzger, 287/39, 148/80. *Amazons*, e.g. Oxford, 1917.61. *ARV*, 876/1; Metzger, 327/44. *Ethiopians*, Berlin, 3237, *Greek Theatre Production*, no. A10. Metzger, 340/70. Pickard-Cambridge, *Festivals*, fig. 164. Perhaps cf. Antiphanes, 36K.

[2] Cf. above, p. 16. On Philoxenus, cf. *Later Greek Comedy*, 19 ff. On Zeuxis, see Lucian, *Zeuxis*, 3 (Overbeck, 1663).

flattery): of this we have at least two parodies in comedy—the monstrous dish at the end of the *Ecclesiazusae* and an oracular recital of aphrodisiacs in the *Phaon*.[1] We shall have a little more to say later of the subjects of lyric poetry but we cannot say more of their style. We must accept the probability that the curious dissonance between exotic affectation and extreme realism is not confined to Timotheus, since we know that Aristotle regarded Philoxenus, whose fragments only show the rich style, as representing men worse than ourselves. This strain of realism would be sufficient to secure Plato's disapproval, and we do not know of any virtues to urge on the other side.

Tragedy[2] was immensely popular and spread beyond Athens and the local theatres in Attica to Greek cities elsewhere, as the many South Italian vase-pictures of tragic scenes testify. Tragic poets, when they had made their name in Athens, made large sums of money by touring other Greek cities. The tragic actor Theodorus subscribed no less than 70 drachmae to the rebuilding of the temple of Apollo at Delphi, and this perhaps implies that Delphi already provided some sort of protection for actors on their travels, such as we know was later guaranteed by a decree of the Amphictyonic Council. Both in Athens and South Italy old tragedies as well as new tragedies were produced in the fourth century. When therefore Plato attacked fifth-century tragedy, he was not attacking something which was dead and out of date when he wrote. Revivals of Aeschylus had already taken place in the fifth century and from 386 an old tragedy was revived each year at the City Dionysia. When Plato quoted Aeschylus' *Niobe*, *Semele*, and *Hoplon Krisis* in the *Republic*,[3] he was quoting plays which his readers would know, and the evidence of vase-

---

[1] *Rep.* 390 a 10; *Gorgias*, 502; *Eccl.* 1168; Plato, 173K.

[2] Vitucci, *Dioniso*, 7 (1939), 200, 312, gives evidence for tragedy in the fourth century at Peiraeus, Icaria, Eleusis, Aixone, Acharnae. For poets' successes see Plato, *Laches*, 183a. For Theodorus, Tod, *Greek Historical Inscriptions*, ii, no. 140, l. 67. See also *Hermes*, 82 (1954), 294.

[3] *Rep.* 379e, 391e, 381d, 383b, quotations of Aeschylus; 395d–e, Euripidean heroines. Cf. *Frogs*, 1043, 1080.

painting gives us eight further Aeschylean revivals. Of Sophocles we know much less. The evidence is fullest for Euripides, and Euripides interests us most, because, when Plato forbade his guardians to imitate a woman abusing her husband, or sick, or in love, or in travail, he surely had in mind Medea, Alcestis, Phaedra, and Auge. Phaedra and Auge had been named in a similar list of undesirable heroines in Aristophanes' *Frogs*, in which Stheneboea (who tried to seduce Bellerophon) and Canace (who was raped by her brother) were added. We have evidence that all these plays were revived in the early part of the fourth century, and that (with *Medea* and *Stheneboea*) *Andromeda, Iphigenia in Tauris, Meleager, Oenomaus,* and *Telephus* were particularly popular. Plato's criticisms do not seem to have had any effect on the popularity of Euripides, but perhaps if we look at this list we may suggest that fourth-century audiences were less interested in the errant heroines than in the excitement of the story, scenic effects, good speeches for actors, and what today we call 'theatre'.

These characteristics are obviously present in the *Rhesus*. The arguments[1] for its date are not conclusive, but on balance it seems to me to belong to the early fourth century rather than to the fifth. Clearly we must not judge this play by the same standards as the *Oedipus Tyrannus* or even the *Iphigenia in Tauris*. No character, except the Muse, who has some of the colouring of Homer's Thetis, awakes our sympathy. There are no great thoughts, and no great moments like the recognition scene of the *Oedipus Tyrannus* and the *Iphigenia in Tauris*. It has however merits. The structure is clear—Dolon theme, Rhesus theme, knitting of the two by Odysseus and Diomede, lament for Rhesus; the curious device of answering a strophe in the Hector/Rhesus scene by an antistrophe in the Hector/charioteer scene holds the central section of the play together; the balancing narratives of Rhesus in glory and Rhesus in death are in the best tradition of messenger speeches; Hector, Dolon, Rhesus are three interesting variations of the swashbuckler type with grand speeches to deliver; there is

[1] Cf. most recently A. Lesky, *Gnomon*, 1951, 141 f.; Björck, G., *Arktos*, 1954, 16.

plenty of spectacle seen as well as narrated, and finally the charming naturalism of the anapaestic opening and the dawn chorus.

Another tragedy of this period was the *Andromache* of Antiphon (who was put to death by Dionysius the elder). It is clear from two passages of Aristotle[1] that Andromache tried to save her son by giving him to another woman to bring up. As we know that there was a tragedy in which Astyanax was hidden with shepherds but ultimately discovered by Odysseus and killed, it seems probable that this was Antiphon's play. It is possible that we have a papyrus fragment of Andromache's lament for Hector, before she sends Astyanax away; in this dependence on the *Trojan Women* is clear. This seems also to have been a long and exciting play in the Euripidean tradition. Such evidence as we have of early fourth-century tragedy suggests that new composers were dominated by Euripides, but more by the melodramatic than by the psychological plays.

Two Attic vases,[2] painted probably just after the turn of the century, show us the costume of tragedy and satyr play at this time. Except for Silenus and the satyr chorus the costumes are identical on both. Actors and chorus wore clothes covered with elaborate patterns; actors wore ornamented boots; the men's masks had long flowing hair. They were dressed in the richest possible clothing, an exaggeration of the clothes worn by rich men at the time. There is no sign here of the rags of Telephus, which Dicaeopolis borrowed in the *Acharnians*. It is possible that these and other rags which were described in tragedy were not in fact worn, and that it is just this contrast between the imagined rags and the actual stately robes which Aristophanes exploits. In any case realistic words, emotions, and actions were not confined to beggar heroes, and the contrast was there for every spectator

[1] *EE*, 1239 a 37; *NE*, 1159 a 32. See also Servius ad *Aen.* iii, 489; Ribbeck, 159, ix–xi. Terracotta relief, Pickard-Cambridge, *Festivals*, fig. 57. Papyrus, Page, *Greek Literary Papyri*, no. 30.

[2] *Greek Theatre Production*, nos. A12 and 9. (*a*) Würzburg fragments. *ARV*, 965; Pickard-Cambridge, *Festivals*, fig. 40. (*b*) Naples, 3240. Pronomos vase. Here, Pl. 3*b*. *ARV*, 849.

to appreciate. But whereas by these means Euripides said 'Although she is a queen, here and here she is just like you', Aristophanes and Plato said 'Because she is a queen, she is never like you but you must try to be like her'.

5. CONTRASTS AND LEVELS

The contrast between the realistic emotions and actions of the tragic character and his gorgeous appearance on the stage is not unlike the contrast between the comic masks and the disillusioned old man on the Lyme Park relief. Appearance and words belong, as it were, to two different levels. We can see a lower level still if we put tragedy beside mythological comedy. Here we have three levels—the ideal character seen in the rich style of contemporary art and stage production, the naturalistic interpretation by Euripides and his successors (or by lyric poets such as Timotheus), and the caricature (sometimes with a political bias) by the comic poet. We can appreciate the full flavour of the caricature because it is also represented in art. We have a few pictures of comedy on Attic vases of this period and many on South Italian vases from the end of the fifth century onwards.[1] It is at least possible that Pauson started this kind of art. Whether this is true or not, let us look at a couple of instances where this difference of level can be seen.

Spintharus wrote a tragedy or satyr-play called *Herakles Perikaiomenos*, in which presumably Heracles was burnt on the pyre and translated to heaven. Vases of this period often show Heracles going to heaven on a chariot with Athena or Nike as charioteer and Hermes as guide; the hero is sometimes young and sometimes bearded, but the idea of his driving to heaven in youth and glory evidently captured the Athenian imagination. One of

---

[1] Cf. my articles in *CQ*, 42 (1948), 19 f.; *Eph. Arch.*, 1953 (forthcoming); *Greek Theatre Production*, nos. B1–9 (Attic), 32 ff. (South Italian); the vases will all be discussed in A. D. Trendall's forthcoming *Phlyax Vases*.

C

these vases[1] seems to testify to inspiration by a satyr-play, since two satyrs steal Heracles' arms from the pyre, which is being quenched by Arethusa and Premnusia (a spring in Attica). This is the story on the heroic level, since in costume at least the actors of satyr-play and tragedy were indistinguishable. We also have two reflections on the level of comedy. Strattis wrote a *Zopyros Perikaiomenos*; the title is a parody of Spintharus' title. In it someone is told to be brave and singe himself like a moustache; here the allusion is clearly to Dionysius of Syracuse, who had his hair and beard singed by his daughter because he was afraid that a barber might murder him. How far the identification of Dionysius and Heracles was carried we cannot say. A vase[2] by the Nikias painter of the late fifth century also parodies Heracles' drive to heaven, and the source must again be comedy because the figures wear comic costume and comic masks: Heracles has the staring eyes and wide mouth of his comic masks, which are well known from other vases and terracottas; the conflated Athena/Nike who drives him looks like the women of a comic female chorus; his horses are Centaurs (the comedy may have been the *Centaurs* of Nicochares or Apollophanes); and he is preceded by a dancing slave with a torch instead of Hermes.

A second instance is the story of Phaon. Here we cannot name a version in high poetry, but two vases[3] by the Meidias painter depict the story, one painted soon after 420, one at the very end of the fifth century or a little later. The source may be lyric poetry rather than tragedy. We see two moments in the story: Phaon surrounded by nymphs whom he despises, and Phaon reclining in a thicket, while Aphrodite comes to him in a chariot drawn by

---

[1] Munich, 2360. *ARV*, 805/1; Metzger, 210/25. Metzger, *loc. cit.* gives further examples. Cf. here Pl. 4*a*, reproduced from a rather later vase, Birmingham, 1620/85; Heracles has a man and not Athena to drive him.

[2] Here, Pl. 5*a*. Paris, Louvre N 3408. *ARV*, 848/22; Metzger, 212/35; Pfuhl, *MuZ*, fig. 572; Rumpf, *AJA*, 55 (1951), 8.

[3] Florence 81947. *ARV*, 832/4. Palermo, *ARV*, 833. Add a fragment of the early fourth century: Athens, Agora, P10270. Beazley, *AJA*, 54 (1950), 320. Cf. *Studies in Later Greek Comedy*, 18.

Pothos and Himeros. The Meidias painter has used white and gold and all the intricacies of the rich style to beautify his figures. The comic poet Plato produced his *Phaon* in 391. Here we are in the demi-monde of Athens: the hetaira Lais is perhaps one of Phaon's unsuccessful suitors, and Aphrodite has become a procuress telling the women of the chorus what sacrifices they must make to herself and various other fertility spirits if they want to see Phaon. Two terracotta statuettes[1] of comic actors enable us to visualise Aphrodite and Phaon. The woman is grotesquely padded with a comic snub-nosed, wrinkled face; the man is also padded and phallic, with a wide mouth and goggling eyes. The point of any mythological comedy (and about half the known and datable titles of comedy between 420 and 370 are mythological) must be just this contrast between the obscene costumes and earthy sentiments of the comic actors and on the other hand the heroic story which they parody and the rich style in which they often speak. Similarly for the intelligent spectator stage personality contrasted with historical reality when contemporaries were brought on the stage—Socrates in the *Clouds* and Plato in Middle Comedy.

Plato in the *Republic*[2] dismisses comedy contemptuously: its characters are lowborn cowards, who abuse, mock, and speak evil of each other, sometimes drunk and sometimes sober; its laughter is caused by acts which the ordinary man would be ashamed to perform. Yet, whatever damage Aristophanes did to Socrates by the *Clouds*, he is given a not dishonourable place in Plato's *Symposium*, and it is reasonable to see in this an epitaph written by Plato shortly after Aristophanes' death. On the other side, close parallels have been detected between some of the ideas in Aristophanes' last preserved plays and views held by Plato, and it is possible to maintain that, although Aristophanes found admirable comic material for the *Ecclesiazusae* in Plato's communism and for the *Plutus* in Plato's economic interpretation of civilisation, Plato's own demand for honesty and technical skill would not meet with

---

[1] Würzburg. Pickard-Cambridge, *Festivals*, fig. 108*; Bieber, *HT*, fig. 103.
[2] *Rep.* 395c, 606.

Aristophanes' disapproval, so that if anyone were led by the comic representation of communism to find out more about Plato's ideas Aristophanes would not object.[1] Just as, long before, the idea of peace had been put forward by Dicaeopolis dressed in the rags of Telephus with his head on a chopping block, so now in the *Ecclesiazusae* the fun of the women's parliament and the comic consequences of communism are the means of putting forward a demand for efficient and honest government; in the *Plutus* the fantastic figure of Poverty, a cross between a tragic Fury and a landlady, preaches an unpleasant but wholesome doctrine. This serious purpose is the other term of the contrast, which Plato omits to mention in the *Republic*.

Greeks were accustomed to view things on different levels, heroic appearance and human emotions, the same story in tragedy and in comedy. The tragic scene itself was divided into three physical levels, which corresponded to three levels in the rank of the characters—gods on the roof, heroes on the low stage, chorus (who formed a link between heroes and audience) in the orchestra. This way of looking at heroic stories passed from the tragic stage to the artist, and we can quote many pictures of this time in which we can divide the figures into divine onlookers, heroic actors, and human onlookers or chorus.[2] I am going to discuss an example with only two levels, because the subject is one of those mentioned by Plato as objectionable.[3] 'We shall not commend a poet if he says that the Strife (*Eris*) and Judgment of the goddesses was brought about by Themis and Zeus.' The subject is common in vase-painting of our period; the poem in question may be the *Cypria*, but some recent poem is more likely and the fact that one of the vase-paintings includes a tripod suggests that it was painted

---

[1] Cf. *Studies in Later Greek Comedy*, 34f.

[2] e.g. (*a*) gods; Heracles sacrificing; attendants. Leningrad, 43 f. *ARV*, 852/1; Metzger, 194/10; Schefold, *U.*, figs. 70–72; E. Hooker, *JHS*, 70 (1950), 36. (*b*) gods; Hermes, Io, Argus; satyrs. *ARV*, 871/3; Metzger, 338/68. (*c*) Hermes, Aphrodite; Cepheus, Andromeda, Perseus; Ethiopian woman. Berlin, 3237. Cf. above p. 29 n. 1. (*d*) gods; Myrtilus, Oenomaus, Pelops, Hippodamia; attendants. Naples, 2200. *ARV*, 879/1; Metzger, 321/37.   [3] *Rep.* 379e.

in celebration of a victory with a chorus or a play.[1] The most interesting from our point of view is a picture in the rich style by the Kadmos painter[2] painted at the very end of the fifth century, where the actors, Hera with her maid Hebe, Hermes, Paris, Athena, and Aphrodite, occupy the bottom level; behind and above, partly concealed by a range of mountains, are two chariots: one driven perhaps by Iris and led by Eris, the other led by Themis and driven by Nike and behind it stands Zeus. Eris, Themis, and Zeus are the forces behind the judgment of Paris and the ensuing Trojan war, the king of the gods and two personifications.

Thus the Greeks were used in the theatre and in art to see things on two or more levels, and the levels were not only physically separated but their occupants had different values. Plato may have been influenced by this contemporary method of seeing and interpreting, at least to the extent of knowing that he would be easily understood, when he divided objects of apprehension into different levels with different values in the three successive images of Sun, Line, and Cave in the *Republic* and in the myth of the sea and the parts of the Universe in the *Phaedo*.[3] In the *Republic* Socrates says that though he cannot give an account of the good he can give an account of its very similar offspring the sun. The sun causes the light by which the eyes can see visible things; similarly the good causes truth by which the soul can know concepts. Plato expressly states that he is using an argument by analogy (or proportion): 'the sun is analogous to the good; the

[1] On the Pronomos vase and the Würzburg fragments (here, Pl. 3*b*, and above, p. 32), the tripod (with or without column) clearly indicates victory with chorus, satyr-play or tragedy. The tripod also occurs with Judgment of Paris (Vienna, 1771, *ARV*, 843; Metzger, 270/9), Reconciliation of Apollo and Heracles (above, p. 16 n. 1), Cadmus (Berlin, F2634, *ARV*, 805/22), Eastern scene with Cyrus (above, p. 29 n. 1), Marsyas (Ruvo, Jatta, 1093. *ARV*, 803/1; Metzger, 160/8), etc.

[2] Here, Pls. 4*b* and 5*b*. Leningrad, St. 1807. *ARV*, 804/5; Metzger, 269/5 (see there also list of other representations).

[3] *Rep.* 506, 509, 514; *Phaedo*, 109b. Cf. P. M. Schuhl, *Fabulation platonicienne*, 41 ff.

good has the same relation to mind and concepts in the conceptual world as the sun to sight and phenomena in the visible world.' The relation of the sun to the visible world and its spectator is known; the analogy explains the relation of the good to the conceptual world and the thinker. This first image is first further developed by the Line, which shows the mathematical relationship between the clarity and truth with which four different kinds of objects in the visible and conceptual world are apprehended, and then by the image of the Cave, which by a similar system of related levels explains both the actual and the possible position of the philosopher in the world. Sun, line, and cave have echoes in many other passages of the *Republic* itself, and arguments on very much the same analogical foundation are presented by, for instance, the four arts and four flatteries in the *Gorgias*.[1] The qualitatively different levels are not unlike the levels that we have been considering; what is peculiar to Plato is the use of geometric proportion to tie them together.

6. Gods and Personifications

There are two other elements in the picture of the judgment of Paris which engage our attention: the attitude of Zeus and the personifications. Zeus takes no part and this is the rule now: the gods sit at ease and look on. This detachment of the gods is perhaps most striking in the scenes where Dionysus sits at ease with Ariadne amid the wild revels of satyrs and maenads or moves dreamily through them.[2] Here we can see three levels again; satyrs and maenads are a translation into mythical terms of the carefree komos of mortals,[3] above and through them moves unheeding Dionysus, the source of their joy. And he is now normally young, as he was in Euripides' *Bacchae* and is in the wonderful Praxitelean

[1] *Gorg.* 464.

[2] e.g. back of Pronomos vase, Pickard-Cambridge, *Dithyramb*, etc., fig. 12.

[3] e.g. Uppsala, *ARV*, 966/1; *Dragma*, 565. Heidelberg, Inv. 29.1. *ARV*, 868/3; *Welt der Griechen*, fig. 37.

head in the British Museum.¹ Apollo was normally young in the
fifth century, but he is a mere boy in the lizard-slaying statue
which Praxiteles carved about the end of our period.² Heracles
was normally bearded in the fifth century and is still sometimes so
represented, but very often now he is young and slim;³ he is no
longer the burly athlete but has a supernatural strength in his fine-
drawn beauty. Sometimes this phenomenon is interpreted to mean
that the gods have become more human and nearer humanity.⁴
Undoubtedly some gods are near to mankind: Demeter and Kore
in the mysteries; Asclepius in his cures. But where we see one of
these young gods or heroes with a mortal worshipper at his side
the difference of scale is clear at once.⁵ Their youth expresses
rather the bliss, perfection, and detachment which are predicated
of the divine by the philosophers, translated into the diverse
human forms of the legendary gods, whom alone sculptors and
painters can represent.

If the gods have now detached themselves from the human
scene, artists and writers introduce another kind of being as an
audience for the gods, as intermediaries between gods and men,
or as associates of men. These are personifications. Some of them
are very old but many of them are new, and they have been used
since the late fifth century in great profusion. Their status varies
from deity to hypostatised abstract according to the will of their
user. Their use varies between persuasion and explanation. In the
Judgment of Paris which we have illustrated Eris and Themis are
traditional personifications which go back to the *Cypria*, but presumably also appeared in the artist's immediate source. They

---

¹ *Bacch.* 453 f. British Museum, 1554, here Pl. 6.   ² Richter, figs. 637–5.

³ e.g. cf. H. with Hesperides (above, p. 14 n. 2), driving to heaven (above,
p. 34 n. 1), with Deianira (reverse of New York, 37.11.23, here Pl. 7). Cf. young
Boreas (*ARV*, 872/26; Metzger, 346/83), young Hephaestus with Dionysus
(above, p. 16 n. 1).   ⁴ e.g. by Picard, *IVe*, 11 f.

⁵ e.g. Theseus and worshippers on relief in Louvre 743, Süsserott, *Griechische
Plastik des IVten Jahrh.*, pl. 14/2. Heracles and worshipper on relief in Athens,
NM., Svoronos, no. 1404; Süsserott, *op. cit.*, pl. 14/3. Cf. also the epiphany of
Aphrodite on the red-figured oenochoe, Berlin, F2660. Metzger, 60/9; Schefold,
U., no. 300.

personify the strife of the goddesses and the strife of the Trojan war and the will of Zeus that these things shall come to pass—explanatory certainly but also persuasive, because both strife and Zeus' will are powerful things.

On another vase[1] Clio watches Helen making her toilet to receive Paris; here the personification explains that the love of Paris and Helen will become famous through the ages. Such explanatory personifications are extremely common in the late fifth and early fourth century; particularly they appear as women in the circle of Aphrodite and as maenads in the circle of Dionysus to tell the spectator what are the concomitants or conditions of Dionysiac ecstasy and of the fulfilment of desire. For instance[2] Dionysus may be surrounded by maenads named Peace, Autumn, Brightness, Good Cheer, and Happiness and also by the winged boys, Love, Desire, and Longing. Aphrodite may be accompanied by women named Harmony, Youth, Health, Fair Fame, Amusement, Happiness, Ease, Orderliness, as well as by her usual attendants Persuasion, Love, Desire, Longing. These personifications all tell the spectator something about Dionysus and Aphrodite, or tell us something about themselves, e.g. that Happiness may supervene as a result of Dionysiac ecstasy or of Love. Similarly in the *Symposium*[3] Plato tells us more about Love by giving Eros a new genealogy; he is the child of Poverty and Contriving and in his behaviour takes partly after his mother and partly after his father: he is in fact characterised both as the successful and as the unsuccessful lover. These figures may be old or they may be new. Harmony, Peace, and Youth were already personified in Hesiod; and we have already noticed that Peace was given divine status at Athens in the early fourth century because Peace was so sorely needed. Many of the others are new, as are for instance Tragedy

---

[1] London, British Museum, E226. *ARV*, 842/3; Metzger, 279/30.

[2] The list is compiled from six vases: (*a*) Vienna, 1024, *ARV*, 790/8. (*b*) Providence, 23.324, *ARV*, 801/1. (*c*) Ruvo, Jatta, 1903 (reverse of scene quoted p. 37 n. 1, above), *ARV*, 803/1. (*d*) Athens, NM, 1629, *ARV*, 726/7. (*e*) London, British Museum, E775, *ARV*, 833/14. (*f*) New York, 09.221.40, *ARV*, 840/86.

[3] *Symp.* 203b.

and Comedy,[1] who appear on vases in the company of Dionysus; they are parallels for the personified Philosophy in Isocrates' *Panegyricus* and the personified dramatic poetry whom Plato drove from his ideal state.

Dionysus when he is surrounded by these personifications may be in Delphi or in an anonymous mountain landscape; Aphrodite and her women may be in Cyprus or on Olympus. The Meidias painter[2] introduces Hygieia (Health) into the Garden of the Hesperides, and twice at least Plato seems to be thinking of a new garden of the Hesperides. One is the passage in the *Republic*[3] when Socrates says: 'We must search those craftsmen whose beauty of character enables them to search out the character of the beautiful and shapely, that, as if living in a healthy place, the young may profit from everything, from all the fair works of which something impinges on their sight or hearing, like a Breeze bringing Health from good places, and leads them into likeness and friendship and harmony with fair Reason.' In a new garden of the Nymphs a personified Breeze (like the lovely sea Breeze who sits on a rock by the shore on a South Italian vase of the late fifth century[4]) brings a personified Health to the young and leads them into friendship with a personified Logos, for whom a parallel may be seen in the personified Laws[5] visiting Socrates in prison.

The other passage is the myth of the *Phaedrus*,[6] which must be quoted here although it takes us beyond our period. There the charioteer of the mortal soul after the greatest struggles and labours catches at most a glimpse of Justice herself, Modesty herself and Knowledge herself in their place beyond heaven, though the gods can see them when they will. The Platonic Forms (or Ideas) are thought of as Nymphs in a remote and secret garden, and the soul is likened to the charioteer of a winged chariot drawn

---

[1] Tragedy, Oxford, 534, *ARV*, 732. Comedy, Louvre, G421, *ARV*, 685/1.
[2] Above, p. 14 n. 2.   [3] *Rep.* 401b.
[4] Sydney, 53.30, to be published by A. D. Trendall, who compares E. *Hec.* 444.
[5] *Crito*, 50.
[6] *Phaedr.* 248. Cf. now B. Schweitzer, *Platon und die bildende Kunst der Griechen*, 61 ff.

by two unlike horses, one characterised as brave and honourable and the other as sensual and passionate. If the 'place beyond heaven' reminds us of the garden of the Hesperides, the drive to heaven reminds us of Heracles' drive to heaven, and whatever other sources Plato may have drawn on, the pictures of Heracles' drive must have been one and would have made the interpretation clear and the image vivid.

Plato (like Parmenides before him) took over a popular and often-represented Heracles story and applied it to the soul. Others at the same time allegorised the Heracles stories or told new stories about Heracles. The sophist Prodicus[1] (probably in the late fifth century) told how Heracles in his first youth sat pondering his future in a quiet place and was visited by Virtue and Vice; Virtue is characterised as a beautiful girl of noble birth and Vice as a *hetaira*. This myth may have inspired or have been inspired by a picture: on the back of the Musaeus vase in New York[2] the young Heracles is seated on a rock and a beautiful woman displays her charms; the vase-painter has called her Deianira, but I can imagine that Vice looked very like this, and Virtue like the sober woman on the left. In the choice of Heracles Prodicus personified and characterised two abstract ideas to persuade people to live virtuously. Vice is characterised as a prostitute, and this imagery recurs in the *Phaedo*,[3] where the soul is pulled along by the body, swaying about like a drunken prostitute; if however it gets free from savage desires, it can live among the gods.

Another kind of figure in art and literature to which personifications can be assimilated are the Furies and similar grim demons, wild energetic women in short chitons. The passions which capture the citadel of the young man's soul in the *Republic*[4] seem to belong to this class, and in the *Phaedo*[5] the personification of each Pleasure and Pain as a woman holding a nail in her hand to nail the soul to the body must derive from some similar figure from

---

[1] Xen. *Mem.* II, 1, 21.
[2] Here, Pl. 7. Above, p. 14 n. 3. Cf. however, Picard, *RA*, 21, 163.
[3] *Phaedo*, 79 cd; 81a.   [4] *Rep.* 560b.   [5] *Phaedo*, 83d.

the world of the Hades myths. Taken out of their context such figures are a powerful inducement to virtue. The myths about Hades themselves, which occur in several dialogues of Plato (*Gorgias, Phaedo, Republic*), are both persuasive and explanatory. The continued existence of the soul as a person is assumed, and the myths give a reasonable but unverifiable account of its experiences before life and after death. In each case the myth clarifies and therefore helps to establish a position which cannot convincingly be established by argument because it is not amenable to the test of experience. These myths belong to a long tradition of Hades pictures and Hades poetry. An Athenian krater[1] of about 440 B.C. shows Herakles fetching Theseus from the underworld: Palamedes, Ajax, Elpenor, and Meleager are present but also certain nameless Athenians. This clearly illustrates the same kind of belief as Socrates shows in the *Apology* when he hopes to see the heroes after death. In Hades scenes on South Italian vases[2] of the second half of the fourth century we find, besides the well-known heroes, Minos, Rhadamanthys, and Aeacus, who are the judges of the *Gorgias* myth; there they judge in a meadow, which, like the river of the *Phaedo* myth, can also be seen on the vases. The daimon who conducts the souls in the *Phaedo* can be equated with the Furies, the Poinai, and Aika (which presumably means 'torture') on the vases. Besides these Ananke appears on one vase and the Fates can be seen in the Hades scene on a sarcophagus, which may derive from the Nekyia of the painter Nicias:[3] these Plato had introduced in the myth of the *Republic*. Thus the Hades scenes are evidence not only for personifications—the soul, Furies, Necessity, and others, but also for the close interrelation of literature and art.

---

[1] New York, 08.258.21; Beazley, *ARV*, 717/1; Nilsson, *Gesch.* i, pl. 51/1.

[2] A good selection in Guthrie, *Orpheus*, 187 f.; Pickard-Cambridge, *Theatre*, 94 f.

[3] Keil, *Jahreshefte*, 1914, 135 ff.

7. CONCLUSION

We cannot understand the art without the literature or the literature without the art. We can see on one side the consistent rich style of Isocrates and the Meidias painter and on the other the realism of certain sculpted, painted, and written portraits. Between the two stylistic extremes Lysias and Plato seem to us to have achieved a reconciliation, which is hard to detect in the lyric poets and tragedians. But realism in portraiture seems itself to be an example of a way of seeing which we have found in all the arts and in different departments of the arts—seeing in levels or seeing in contrasts. Personifications, which we have just studied, may be used to form such a contrast or to people such a level. They may be contrasted with Aphrodite or Dionysus as followers contrasted with their leaders (in which case they could be translated into prose as the conditions, concomitants, effects, or results of a psychological state), or they may be contrasted as stronger and more permanent with the human beings who are in some way dependent on them. Or they may people a place beyond heaven where they can only be seen with difficulty by mortals, and in this case they may be Platonic Ideas contrasted with the world of becoming and decay.

The words used by Plato for his Ideas, *eidos* and *idea*, probably carried with them some of their original meaning of visible shape when they were first used in the second half of the fifth century for 'kinds' of disease, 'forms' of attack, 'forms' of poetry and other generalities. If they were also used (which we cannot prove) for mathematical figures, they carried with them some of the permanent, hyperphysical reality accredited to mathematical figures. Of the two sorts of words used by Plato for particular ideas, one— e.g. 'the good itself'—by its very form (neuter adjective with definite article) suggests substantial reality, the other, the feminine abstract noun, such as Virtue and Courage, belonged to a long tradition of personifications beginning with such figures as

Homer's Ate in the ninth book of the *Iliad* and greatly extended, as we have seen, in the late fifth century. Plato passionately desired to give ethical universals the same kind of permanent reality as mathematical universals. This was his interpretation of Socrates' message. *Eidos* and *idea* and 'the good itself' all suggested visible reality; and feminine abstracts were already established as personifications in art and literature and could dwell for ever in a garden contrasted with our transitory world.

Much of the early fourth century is in the straight line of development from the fifth century. The political and ethical thought of Plato and Isocrates grew naturally out of the thought of Socrates, Protagoras, and Theramenes. The Eirene, which Cephisodotus carved in 373, is the last of a line of draped female figures which can be traced back through Pheidias to the Argive sculptors of the time of the Persian wars, and the rich style of the early fourth century derived directly from the rich style of the 30's of the fifth. It is unlikely that if we possessed more early fourth-century tragedy we should observe a clear break with Euripides any more than the *Ecclesiazusae* and the *Plutus* show an essential break with Old Comedy. Yet this is also a new period which shows the beginnings of classical painting, of individual characterisation in sculpture and comedy, and the achievement of Isocratean prose and Platonic philosophy—a new Athens, ready for the youthful Aristotle.

III

Art and Literature in Aristotle's Athens

1. POLITICAL LITERATURE AND ART

ARISTOTLE arrived in Athens in 367 and remained there for twenty years until Plato's death. He returned in 335 and only left again in 323 shortly before his own death. Our period may be taken as the forty-five years from 367 to 322. At its start the Second Athenian Confederacy was still in existence with Timotheus as a successful general, and Plato's Sicilian experiment was one symptom of Athenian interest in the West. The Confederacy came to an end in the disastrous Social War of 357–5. From that time the rising power of Philip of Macedon was felt, and Athens was finally defeated at the battle of Chaeronea in 338. Philip was succeeded by Alexander, who then launched his Asiatic campaigns and died in 323. Athens started the period as a powerful and independent city, and ended it with an oligarchic constitution imposed by Antipater and maintained by his garrison. On the whole the changes in art and literature cannot be attributed to political events and throughout the period Athens maintained her position as the intellectual centre of Greece. But the orators were also politicians, comedy and tragedy were produced at public festivals, and some traces of official art can be seen.

Isocrates' school continued on the same lines, as the *Antidosis* shows, and his style did not change significantly, but the buoyancy of the *Panegyricus* gave place to the disillusioned conservatism of the *Peace* and the treachery of his letter to Philip, proving Philip's title as a descendant of Heracles to be overlord of the Greeks. Of his pupils Theodectes, Astydamas, and Lycurgus will engage our attention later. We know less of the Academy's effect on internal politics, but Hyperides, Chabrias, and Phocion were all numbered among its pupils.[1] After Plato's death Speusippus seems to have vied with Isocrates in currying favour with Philip.[2] A picture of the young Academician in politics is given by the comic poet Ephippus:[3] 'he consorts with Art—the Art of making money by speaking, and cannot say anything incautious'; his hair is carefully cut, his beard is long, his sandal straps are neatly plaited, his toe-nails are trimmed, his cloak is imposingly draped, and he makes a noble figure leaning on his stick, but when he opens his mouth, nothing comes out but a cliché. He apparently had not followed the rules laid down by Plato in the *Phaedrus* on the necessity of understanding the psychology of the audience. The discussion of rhetoric in the *Phaedrus* shows that the teaching of the Academy had some bearing on practical politics and Aristotle was teaching practical rhetoric before Plato's death.[4] In the same period Demosthenes developed a prose perfectly adapted both to his democratic idealism and to his passionate denigration of his enemies. For the first time perhaps personal invective filled a large part of Athenian speeches,[5] set off by an idealisation of the past, which in different guises was common to Demosthenes, Isocrates and Plato;[6] but whereas Isocrates and Plato praised the restraint of early democracy, Demosthenes praised rather its sense of responsibility.

Some of the violence of Aristophanic comedy seems to have spilled over into political eloquence; but comedy also could still be political and it is not always easy to decide whether a comic poet is borrowing from an orator or an orator from a comic poet.

---

[1] On the political activity of the Academy, cf. P. M. Schuhl, *REG*, 59 (1946), 46.

[2] *F. Gr. Hist.*, no. 59; cf. M. P. Nilsson, *Cults, etc. and Politics in Ancient Greece*, 103.

[3] fr. 14K (*Nauagos*), cf. *Studies in Later Greek Comedy*, 51 f., L. Radermacher, *Artium Scriptores*, 187.

[4] Cf. below, p. 59.   [5] Cf. below, p. 98.

[6] Cf. particularly Isocrates in the *Areopagiticus*, vii, 37 ff.; Plato in the *Laws*, 698–700.

Ephippus in his *Geryon*[1] satirised foreign policy in the early sixties, when Athens was trying to make alliances with Macedon and Dionysius of Syracuse and to raise revolts in the East against Persia: he pictured the Mediterranean as a vast cooking pot round which the different nations, directed by the Athenian fleet, were lighting fires to cook a fish for the triple-bodied monster Geryon. Later, in the years before Chaeronea, Timocles[2] called Demosthenes 'the son of Briareus who eats catapult shot and spears, who hates words, who never yet made an antithesis but has Ares in his eyes', implying thereby that Demosthenes loved words, made a famous antithesis in the debate about Halonnesus and was a coward. Timocles told his audience that all Demosthenes' war talk amounted to nothing. In these years the comic poets were divided into those who favoured Philip and those who hated him.

Comedy always abused. Painting and sculpture praised when they were commanded. Two Athenian battles were celebrated in painting during the sixties: Pamphilus[3] painted the battle of Phlius in 366 and Euphranor[4] the battle of Mantinea in 362. Euphranor's picture was one of three in the Stoa of Zeus: besides the battle, he painted the Twelve Gods and a picture of Theseus with Democracy and Demos. The set of pictures seems to have been a celebration of the general peace achieved for a moment by the Mantinea campaign—peace won with the will of the gods by the Athenian democracy in battle. The tradition of Athenian democracy, said the picture, goes back to heroic times; perhaps Theseus was painted giving Democracy to Demos as a bride.

Theseus had been the hero of the Athenian democracy since the time of Cleisthenes. In 370 Isocrates had said that Theseus gave the *demos* full powers over the constitution but they demanded that he should rule alone; in 339 he changed the formula and said that Theseus handed over the government to the multitude; later

---

[1] fr. 5K (*Geryones*), cf. *Studies in Later Greek Comedy*, 40 f.
[2] fr. 12K (*Heroes*).   [3] Pliny, *NH*, xxxv, 76 (Overbeck 1753).
[4] Pliny, *NH*, xxxv, 129; Pausanias, i, 3, 3 (full references, Overbeck 1790–6). Cf. H. A. Thompson, *Hesperia*, 21 (1952), 50.

still Theseus was called by Theophrastus the first victim of ostracism.[1] Euphranor's picture agrees with and perhaps inspired Isocrates' second formulation. Readers of Aristophanes will find nothing strange in the personification of Demos, and in the fourth century he appears as a heroic bearded figure on the reliefs which surmount Athenian public documents. It is peculiarly appropriate that a personified Democracy should place a wreath on the head of Demos on a relief[2] at the top of a decree which was passed within two years of Chaeronea and was directed against any attempt to overthrow the democracy or set up a tyranny. Democracy had also a statue at which sacrifices were made; and about 338 the comic poet Heniochus described in a prologue (spoken perhaps by a personification of Olympia) the Cities, who formed the chorus, and said: 'two women are always there to disturb them. One is called Democracy and the other Aristocracy; these two have often made the Cities brawl.'[3] Thus personification continues to be used as a convenient means of explaining and persuading. Of this more will be said later.

Some thirty years after Euphranor's celebration of Athenian democratic triumph, at a time when statues and pictures of Alexander and his family were appearing in all Greek cities, the statesman Lycurgus rebuilt the theatre of Dionysus in stone and erected bronze statues of the three great tragedians, Aeschylus, Sophocles, and Euripides.[4] There is some evidence that the appearance of tragic actors was changed at the same time:[5] new masks were introduced with a tower of formalised hair over the forehead, which gave the characters a more stately appearance and removed them further from everyday life. Athens in the cruel years after Chaeronea must be reminded of her past glory, and a worthy staging of classical tragedy could contribute to this memory. In his one surviving speech Lycurgus quoted a long passage from

[1] Isocrates, x, 36; xii, 128; Theophrastus, *Char.* 26, 6 with fr. 131.
[2] Athens, Agora I 6524. Here, Pl. 8. *Hesperia*, 21 (1952), 355, no. 5.
[3] Statues: *IG*, II², 1011, 1496/131. Cf. *Ath. Mitt.* 1941, 225. Heniochus, 5K.
[4] Cf. below, p. 64.
[5] Cf. *JHS*, 71 (1951), 229, and my forthcoming *Greek Theatre Production.*

Euripides' *Erechtheus* to contrast the heroism of the Athenian princess with the treachery of Leocrates, the contemporary whom he was attacking. How exactly Aristotle stood to Lycurgus we cannot tell, but the canonisation of the classical tragedians in his *Poetics* was perfectly attuned to Lycurgus' programme, and it is reasonable to suppose that Aristotle, under the disadvantage of being established in Athens with the patronage of Alexander, gladly lectured on a theme which would show his sympathy with Athenian policy and express his gratitude for twenty years of training in Athens.

But could a pupil of Plato honestly praise the plays and poets whom Plato had expelled with contumely from his Ideal City? The attempt to answer this question will take us below the surface of official art and literature (and of the official aspects of art and literature). We have to ask how philosophy itself changed between the writing of the *Republic* and the writing of the *Poetics*, and what interaction is observable between philosophy on the one hand and art and literature on the other.

2. Aristotle and Plato

Three suggestions may be made and together they account for the position which Aristotle took up in the *Poetics*. First, art and literature themselves changed. The detailed evidence for this must be postponed for the moment but two important points may be briefly mentioned here. In painting both the rich style, which covered the drapery with patterns and folds and the figures with golden ornaments, and the gradations of colour used in the comparatively new technique of shading were apt to obscure the structure of the single figure and perhaps the composition of the whole picture. About 370 a reaction in favour of clearer outlines and therefore more emphatic composition can be seen in vase-painting (the style called Kertch, because many of the vases were found in South Russia) and has been attributed to the influence of the Sicyonian painter Pamphilus, who insisted on careful draughtsmanship. Of composition in literature we shall have much to say later. The other point is a new idealism in representing heroic figures, which sounds almost like an attempt to meet Plato's criticisms: Euphranor, who painted the pictures in the Stoa of Zeus, was regarded as the first to 'express the dignity of heroes' and his statue of Hephaestus did not show the god's lameness.[1] Two contemporary tragedians are quoted by Aristotle[2] as having produced noble examples of heroes striving against grief and pain; one of these two, Theodectes, gave his Philoctetes a wounded hand instead of the traditional wounded foot; he therefore, like Euphranor's Hephaestus, was not lame, and we can see a similar desire to preserve heroic dignity in both. Aristotle had therefore some contemporary justification for asserting that tragedy represented men who were better than ourselves, and thereby disposed of one of Plato's objections.

More important, however, than the movement of poets and artists towards the philosophers is the movement of the philosophers towards the poets and artists. This was both a general change of position and at the same time a particular reorientation with regard to tragedy and rhetoric, influenced, as I shall suggest, by the move of the elder Theodectes from Isocrates to the Academy. Just as valuable contemporary evidence for the teaching of practical rhetoric in the Academy is provided by the fragment which has been quoted from Ephippus, so a fragment of another comic poet, Epicrates,[3] illustrates this more general change of position: 'At the Panathenaea I saw a crowd of youths in the gymnasia of the Academy and I heard them saying the most extraordinary and absurd things. They were defining natural things and distinguishing the life of animals, the growth of trees, and kinds of vegetables, and then they examined a pumpkin to try

[1] Pliny, *NH*, xxxv, 128; Dio Chrys. 37, 43 (Overbeck 1802, 1800).

[2] *NE*, 1150 b 9 with commentators *ad loc*. Philoctetes of Theodectes and Cercyon in *Alope* of Carcinus.

[3] Epicrates, fr. 11K. Cf. *Studies in Later Greek Comedy*, 54, and most recently J. Skemp, *Plato's Statesman*, 68 ff. Cf. also J. Stenzel, *Plato's Method of Dialectic*, 124; F. Solmsen, *Entwicklung der aristotelischen Logik und Rhetorik*, 54 f.

and classify it. . . . One said it was a round vegetable, one that it was a grass, and one that it was a tree.' A Sicilian doctor laughed them to scorn, but 'Plato very gently and quite undisturbed told them to define its classification again, and they went on with their divisions'. The doctor presumably laughed because they did not dissect the pumpkin, but whether they had a real pumpkin or not, they were at least discussing real pumpkins, and this was the discipline of the Academy at a time soon after Aristotle's arrival.

The last word of the quotation 'they went on with their divisions' is the technical term for the method of dichotomy, which Plato employs in the later dialogues to obtain definitions. Dichotomy is a mathematical method devised to ensure that nothing is left out in a definition. To define a particular activity, e.g. angling, the most general relevant class of activities, here what a Greek calls *techne*, is taken and represented by a vertical line, which is divided into arts of making and arts of possessing; the lower half (arts of possessing) is subdivided into exchanging and capturing, and so on until angling is found and can be defined by its genus and successive differentiae. This procedure was the origin of two quite different procedures: one is the Aristotelian syllogism, which can be constructed from three stages of the division, the other biological classification, of which Epicrates gives us an example. Aristotle easily showed the disadvantages of rigid dichotomy for this purpose, and proposed a classification into genera, between which the likenesses are analogies, and within genera into species, between which the differences are quantitative rather than qualitative.[1] His word for species is *eidos* (Plato's word for his eternal Ideas), and *eidos* in this sense only exists when informing matter, just as matter only exists when informed. This development had important consequences for arts as well as science.

This revolution in thought, which Aristotle alone of Plato's pupils could push to its conclusion, took place in the years when they were together in the Academy. Preliminary stirrings can be seen in the *Phaedo* and the *Republic*, but on the whole it is true to

[1] *de part. An.* i, 4, 644a 12.

say that in the early dialogues the Ideas coexist on one level, while people and things grow and decay on another level. The method of dichotomy changed the relation of the Ideas to each other by arranging them in a hierarchy and emphasised the lowest, indivisible Idea, the species which informs matter; but there is, I think, no evidence that Plato himself realised that his eternal Ideas had thereby changed their meaning or that biological classification could be an end in itself. He was however now much more interested in the historical, sensible world than before. The exposition which forms so large a part of the later Platonic dialogues is factual in a new way. In the *Phaedrus* the chief teachers of rhetoric are named and labelled. The *Laws* quotes the past history of Athens, the Peloponnese, and Persia, and thus fixes the degeneration of constitutions in time: it is an extension of the same process when the ideal state is put into Athenian prehistory in the *Critias*.[1] Even the myths of the *Timaeus*, *Laws*, and *Politicus* owe more to mathematicians, scientists, and astronomers.[2] It is difficult to be rid of the impression that the old Plato is translating the work of a team of technicians into terms of a mythical cosmogony which may be intelligible to the educated Athenian.

The biological works are evidence enough for Aristotle's shift of interest. This new attitude to the natural world had several results, which are directly relevant to our subject. Aristotle often speaks of Nature as a person, and in so doing is echoing the age-old assumption of a world being, which had been progressively modernised through the history of Greek thought by earlier thinkers from Thales to Diogenes of Apollonia. Plato speaks of the Demiurge; Aristotle calls Nature the Demiurge (or Craftsman).[3] For Aristotle the world is composed of two sorts of works, the works of *techne* (art) and the works of *physis* (nature), and the latter are constantly explained by the analogy of the former. The

[1] *Laws*, 687–700. On the *Critias* see Broneer, *Hesperia*, Supplt. viii, 47; Herter, *Rh. Mus.* 96 (1953), 1.

[2] Cf. P. M. Schuhl, *Fabulation platonicienne*, 89 f. on *Politicus*; 106 f. on *Laws*, 903–4; W. Theiler, *Teleologische Naturbetrachtung*, 75 f. on *Timaeus*, 33, 45, 77.

[3] *de part. An.* 645 a 8, cf. Theiler, *op. cit.*, 85.

analogy is often with craftsmanship rather than with art—with the architect, the sword-maker, and the smith—but not exclusively. In the discussion of Substance in the sixth book of the *Metaphysics*[1] Aristotle's first example of matter, form, and product is bronze, the 'sensible shape', and the statue. Here the example is drawn from sculpture. So also in the act of generation *physis* is described not only as a carpenter using a tool but in certain cases as a modeller using her own hands, while he says of the growth of the embryo:[2] 'everything is defined first by outlines, and later takes on colours, hardness, and softness, just as if nature, who constructs it, were a painter. For painters first draw the lines and then cover the painted animal with colours.' More important still, when he is criticising the doctrines of Speusippus in book *N* of the *Metaphysics*,[3] he says: 'the observed facts show that nature is not a series of episodes like a bad tragedy.' The dramatic poet joins the other artists and craftsmen in providing an illustration for the supposed working of nature.

If Jaeger's argument is right and book *N* was written soon after Aristotle left Athens, organic composition of tragedy was already part of Aristotelian poetic theory before he left Athens and he could refer to an 'episodic tragedy' and be understood. To this subject we shall return later. Another extremely important consequence of the analogy which Aristotle draws between the processes of art and the processes of nature, is that he transfers from biology to literary and artistic criticism the idea of organic growth: 'after it had been through many changes, tragedy stopped changing because it had attained its own nature.'[4] In the *Poetics* we have parts of such a sketch of the history of tragedy from its origin in the improvisations of the leaders of the dithyramb: we hear for instance that Aeschylus increased the number of actors from one to two and decreased the songs of the chorus and made the dialogue the protagonist. A stage before Aeschylus is

[1] *Met.* 1029 a 3.   [2] *de gen. An.* 730 b 7; 743 a 23.
[3] *Met.* 1090 b 19, cf. W. Jaeger, *Aristotle*, 224 ff.
[4] *Poetics*, 1449 a 15, cf. *Symb. Osl.* 29 (1952), 22.

preserved by Themistius,[1] who tells us that according to Aristotle Thespis invented the prologue and the speeches. This note presumably, like the theory of organic composition quoted in the *Metaphysics*, comes from an early work on literary criticism: we know that the dialogue *On Poets*[2] mentioned Alexamenus as the inventor of the Socratic dialogue, and it may be that Aristotle treated at some length there the growth of literary forms. Whether we regard this transference of the biological concept of growth to literature as justifiable or not, we cannot doubt its importance in the later history of criticism; and we may reasonably suppose that the beginnings of historical criticism—the explanation of a passage in terms of other work by the same author or of the practices current in his own day, and the careful collection of historical records about literature—beginnings which can also be traced back beyond the *Poetics* to the dialogue *On Poets* and to the preliminary studies for that dialogue (e.g. *Homeric Problems* and similar works), are the outcome of the same biological view of literature.

Aristotle's conception of species may help us also to understand his assertion of the universality of poetry. Poetry is more 'philosophical and serious than history' because instead of recording the acts of individuals it tells the probable or necessary actions of a certain type of man; the chance names of characters in comedy show that comedy has this purpose, and the tragic poet is advised to start by setting out the bare bones of his story in universal terms.[3] The theory is a direct answer to Plato; poetry is not an imitation of an imitation of a reality but creates a new reality, which is itself a union of individual and universal. I believe that Aristotle here views a play in rather the same way as he views Socrates or a particular house. Socrates is the universal, man (the species), realised and individualised by this matter. The particular

---

[1] 316 d, cf. Pickard-Cambridge, *Dithyramb*, 100.

[2] fr. 72 Rose, cf. also fr. 676, 677. On the dialogue see Rostagni, *RFIC*, 54 (1926), 433; 55 (1927), 140; L. Alfonsi, *RIFC*, 70 (1942), 193.

[3] *Poetics*, 1451 b 5, 1455 a 34.

house is the universal, house, realised and individualised by these bricks and mortar. The *Iphigenia in Tauris* is similarly a universal story realised and individualised by these episodes, verses, and names.

So far biology has been made to account for a good deal of Aristotle's outlook on tragedy. *Mimesis* he can defend as being a natural human activity and a method of obtaining knowledge, but he must surely have developed this somewhere at greater length than he does in our *Poetics*.[1] He can also defend the emotionalism of tragedy, which Plato regarded as dangerous, by the theory of *katharsis*, or the purging of emotions by pity and fear; this he seems to have elaborated in the dialogue *On Poets*.[2]

The assumptions of the *Poetics* are fundamentally different from the assumptions of the *Republic*, our last lighthouse in the history of Greek aesthetics, and much of it is a point for point reply to the *Republic*. In the *Republic* the dramatic poet and the illusionistic artist are imitators of what is itself an imitation and incapable of giving knowledge; for Aristotle, works of art are the products of *techne*, a creative activity which is parallel to and a valuable analogy for the creative activity of nature; imitation (mimesis) is a specifically human method of learning, and poetry is nearer philosophy than history because it exemplifies the working of laws. Plato said that the characters of tragedy behaved unworthily of their heroic status. Aristotle asserted that they are better than we are. Plato feared the emotional effect on the audience; Aristotle defined tragedy as producing a *katharsis* of pity and fear and thereby justified its existence in the state.

We have already found evidence that some of Aristotle's fundamental positions were established long before the probable date of our *Poetics* and therefore are likely to belong to his first Athenian period. One of these, which has no connection with the study of nature, is the theory of *katharsis*. To achieve this effect tragedy must be composed to arouse the appropriate emotions. It is not simply an organic composition (which can be compared

[1] *Poetics*, 1448 b 5. [2] Cf. Rostagni, *RIFC*, 54 (1926), 464 on fr. 81.

with the work of Nature) but an organic composition composed to have a particular effect on the listening audience. The phraseology of the passage in the *Poetics* in which Aristotle demands that the plot shall be an organic whole echoes Plato's *Phaedrus*.[1] There Plato is discussing organic unity in a speech; he quarrels with the contemporary rhetoricians because they teach the preliminaries of rhetoric and not rhetoric itself. He goes on later:[2] ' "Suppose anyone were to go to Sophocles and Euripides and say that he knew how to make long speeches on a trivial subject and trivial speeches on an important subject and speeches calculated to raise pity or fear or any other emotion and that he thinks by teaching this he is giving instruction in the art of tragedy." "I think, Socrates, the tragic poets would laugh to scorn anyone who thought that tragedy was anything else but the fitting together of these speeches so that they blended with each other and formed a whole." ' There are several points to note here: first, Plato demands organic composition in a tragedy as in a speech, and in this foreshadows Aristotle, although we may suppose that the contrast between the universality of such a tragic plot and the particularity of history is Aristotle's own and that the comparison with organic nature means more for Aristotle than for Plato. Plato himself is not concerned here with the purpose or the status of tragedy; he introduces it as another kind of rhetoric as he had previously in the *Gorgias*.[3] Secondly, Plato's account of tragic speeches corresponds (with one omission) to Aristotle's account of *dianoia* in the *Poetics*:[4] 'ability to prove and disprove, to stir the passions of pity, fear, anger, etc., to magnify or minimise any event.' *Dianoia* Aristotle expressly says belongs rather to the science of rhetoric, and in fact in this theory the actor is conceived as a rhetorician swaying an audience (the smaller audience in the *orchestra* is not distinguished from the larger audience in the auditorium): such speeches clearly were favourites with the actors and might, as Aristotle saw, lead to the distortion of the whole.

[1] *Poetics*, 1450 b 25 ff.; *Phaedrus*, 264b.
[2] *Phaedrus*, 268c.   [3] *Gorgias*, 502.   [4] *Poetics*, 1456 a 37.

Two important elements in Aristotle's *Poetics*—organic composition and *dianoia*—lead us back to the *Phaedrus* and the discussion of rhetoric there.

Rhetoric and tragedy were combined in the person of one man, Theodectes, whom tradition connects with Plato and Aristotle as well as with his teacher Isocrates. I propose to argue that this man became closely associated with Plato at about the time that Plato wrote the *Phaedrus* and strongly influenced Aristotle's poetic theory as well as his rhetorical theory (to which I shall return later). To show this I must try and clarify the complicated relations between Plato and Isocrates during the last twelve years or so of Plato's life. Full weight must be given to the closing words of the *Phaedrus*, which may be paraphrased thus: 'Isocrates has a much better mind than Lysias and his like; I should not be surprised if he goes on to something much bigger than anything he has attempted so far. For there is a kind of inborn philosophy in him.' It is not a question only or primarily of composition but also of subject-matter and audience. Plato demands knowledge in the orator and the power to adapt his speech to the psychology of the particular audience; the second demand is not very different from Isocrates' theory of *kairos* (the ability to seize an opportunity and exploit it).

It is certainly possible that Isocrates' more kindly reference to the Academy in the *Antidosis*,[1] which he wrote in 353, was prompted by Plato's reference to Isocrates at the end of the *Phaedrus*. The latter should be taken at its face value, and if we remember the fundamental difference between the two men's conception of philosophy it is difficult to see how Plato could have credited Isocrates with more than 'a sort of philosophy'. Nor could Isocrates well grant more than that a short flirtation with Platonic philosophy could do no serious damage. Another passage in the *Antidosis*,[2] in which Isocrates first states his superiority to the experts in law and then to those who write exhortations to Virtue and Wisdom (*phronesis*), has been referred first to the

[1] xv, 261 f.   [2] xv, 79 f. 84 f.

work which was going on in the Academy on the *Laws* and secondly to Aristotle's *Protrepticus*. The *Protrepticus* was an exhortation to the philosophical life (in the true sense) addressed to a Cyprian prince, and quite probably contained some criticism of Isocrates, who likewise addressed Cyprian princes, Evagoras and Nicocles.

Aristotle's earliest work on Rhetoric was the dialogue *Grylus*, which must have been published within a reasonable time of the death of Grylus, the son of Xenophon, killed at the battle of Mantinea in 362. We know that Aristotle mentioned the large number of *encomia* on Grylus, and we also know that one of them was written by Isocrates. It seems at least possible that Aristotle criticised the writers of these *encomia* in the same way as Lysias is criticised in the *Phaedrus*. According to Quintilian[1] Aristotle 'in his passion for research thought out in the *Grylus* certain arguments of his usual subtlety to show that rhetoric was not an art, and yet he also wrote three books on the art of rhetoric'. Quintilian marks a break between the *Grylus* and the *Rhetoric*. The same break is marked by Philodemus, Cicero, and again by Quintilian himself elsewhere;[2] according to them Aristotle was moved by the success of Isocrates to abandon both his attacks on rhetoric and his praise of the contemplative life to teach rhetoric, introducing his afternoon lectures with a parody of Euripides: 'It is base to be silent and allow Isocrates to speak.' The break must have been before Aristotle left Athens in 347. He was answered by Isocrates' pupil Cephisodorus, who wrote four books *Against Aristotle*. He started with Plato's Ideas.[3] This proves, as has been seen, that Cephisodorus wrote while Aristotle was still a Platonist. Such an opening would not be irrelevant if Aristotle had taken the line which he takes at the beginning of the *Rhetoric*:[4]

[1] Aristotle, fr. 69R = Quintilian, ii, 17, 14.

[2] Philodemus, *Vol. Rhet.* ii, 36; Cicero, *de Or* iii, 35, 141; Quintilian, iii, 1, 14.

[3] Eusebius, *Praep. Ev.* xiv, 6. Cf. L. Radermacher, *Artium Scriptores*, 197 f.

[4] Particularly *Rhet.* 1354 b 16. Note also the echo of Plato, *Gorgias*, 464c, in 1356 a 27.

rhetoric is complementary to dialectic; it has no concern with the emotions or disposition of the audience; its purpose is to provide *enthymemes*, based on general arguments, which prove that something has happened or not happened. But when did Aristotle formulate these views, which he has left in the *Rhetoric*, although they are incompatible with all his later discussions about fitting the speech to the character of the audience, stirring emotions, and adapting style to different parts of the speech? This strict position of Aristotle's is also incompatible with the *Phaedrus*, where Socrates says that the function of oratory is to influence men's souls and therefore the orator must know what types of souls there are and by what kinds of speech each is persuaded. A possible explanation of these facts is that Aristotle's extreme position, which he has incorporated in the introduction of the *Rhetoric*, dates from the time of the *Grylus* and was answered soon after by Cephisodorus. The two old masters, Plato and Isocrates, unperturbed by the fierceness of their pupils, nodded politely at one another in the *Phaedrus* and the *Antidosis*. On this view the *Phaedrus*[1] was written between 362, the earliest possible date for the *Grylus*, and 353, the date of the *Antidosis*. It seems at least likely that Aristotle was employed in collecting the historical data about past rhetoricians for the *Phaedrus* and that he published this in his *Synagoge Technon*. Aristotle was thus directed to a much more practical view of rhetoric, partly by the *Phaedrus*, partly perhaps because the Academy needed to compete with Isocrates on more equal terms.

The essential break comes between Aristotle's *Grylus*, written in the late sixties and in the spirit of the *Gorgias*, denying that rhetoric could be an art, and Plato's *Phaedrus*, which, with its insistence on composition and on the need for understanding the psychology of the audience, looks forward to the teaching of prac-

---

[1] This dating is in substantial agreement with W. Jaeger, *Paideia*, iii, 146 n. 109; the philosophical grounds for late dating will be found in O. Regenbogen, *Misc. Ac. Ber.* 1950, 201. On Aristotle's early career with good bibliography, see also P. Moraux, *Les Listes anciennes des ouvrages d'Aristote*, 324.

tical rhetoric in the Academy. We are told that Theodectes, orator and tragic poet, was a pupil of Isocrates, Plato and Aristotle, and he defined the function of the orator entirely in terms of his effect on his audience;[1] composition was part of the doctrine of Isocrates, and his principles of composition are put most clearly in the *Letter to the Children of Jason*, which Jebb dates in 359.[2] In the *Rhetoric* Aristotle both quotes and uses Theodectes.[3] I suggest that Theodectes came to the Academy before Plato wrote the *Phaedrus* and that his presence materially influenced the theories held in the Academy not only on rhetoric but also on tragedy.

Theodectes was then a man at least in his thirties. The two certain points in his life are that he won his first victory with tragedies at the Greater Dionysia in the early sixties and that he visited Halicarnassus soon after the death of Mausolus in 353. The date of his first victory must have been about 368 because the fragmentary inscription lists first Carcinus, whose floruit is given by Suidas as 380–76, then Astydamas, who is recorded by the Parian Marble as having won his first victory in 372, then Theodectes, and finally Aphareus, whose first production was in 369–8.[4] Theodectes cannot therefore have been born later than 390. There is however a difficulty: according to Suidas he died at the age of 41, and according to Plutarch 'Alexander's association with him was due to Aristotle and philosophy', which implies that he was still alive in 340. Two solutions are possible: either Plutarch is not to be taken literally but merely means that Alexander heard much of Theodectes from Aristotle, or the sentence in Suidas 'he died in Athens at the age of 41 in the life time of his father' should be transferred from the elder to the younger Theodectes. If this suggestion of Radermacher's[5] is accepted, it was the

---

[1] Aristotle, fr. 133R.   [2] *Ep.* vi, 8. Jebb, *Attic Orators*, ii, 241.

[3] Cf. Solmsen, *Hermes*, 67 (1932), 147 f.

[4] The list: *IG*, II², 2325; Pickard-Cambridge, *Festivals*, 114; Capps, *AJP*, 1900, 40. On Astydamas, see Wilamowitz, *Aeschylosinterpretationen*, 238. Aphareus: ps. Plut. *Isocrates*, 839d.

[5] L. Radermacher, *op. cit.*, 203.

elder Theodectes who influenced Aristotle and the younger Theodectes who was his pupil and the friend of Alexander. The important and certain point for us, however, is that the elder Theodectes
cannot have been born later than 390 and was producing tragedies
by the time that Aristotle came to Athens. We can therefore now
consider what we know of Greek tragedy in this period and in
particular whether our knowledge helps to explain any of the
puzzling features of the *Poetics*. Later we shall have to examine the
theory of prose style in the *Rhetoric*.

3. TRAGEDY

For the history of tragedy the inscriptions recording the pro-
ductions of the years 341–339[1] are illuminating. They run as follows: in 341 the old tragedy was Euripides' *Iphigenia*, the new
tragedies were Astydamas' *Achilles, Athamas, Antigone*, Euaretus'
Teucer, Achilles, and *X*, Aphareus' *Peliades, Orestes, Auge*. In 340
the satyr-play was Timocles' *Lycurgus*, the old tragedy was
Euripides' *Orestes*, the new tragedies were Astydamas' *Parthenopaeus, Lycaon*, an unknown poet's *X, Phrixus, Oedipus*, and
Euaretus' *Alcmaeon, X*. In 339 the satyr-play was an unknown
poet's *Phorcides*, and the old tragedy was a play by Euripides.
Thus for three years running the old tragedy was a play by
Euripides. On the evidence of vase-paintings the *Iphigenia* is more
likely to have been the *Iphigenia in Tauris* than the *Iphigenia in
Aulis*. But in either case the two titles, *Iphigenia* and *Orestes*, preserved by the inscription belong to the late, exciting and spec-
tacular plays. We can add another: on a relief,[2] which seems to go
back to a memorial erected about 330, Euripides holds the mask of
Heracles and the mask of Lycus is in a basket beside him. The
Hercules Furens is another spectacular, exciting play. The mad
scenes (reported or acted) of the *Iphigenia in Tauris, Heracles*, and
Orestes were great theatre, and some tribute to their popularity

---

[1] *IG*, II², 2320; Pickard-Cambridge, *op. cit.*, 110. Details for tragedy in this
period are given in *Hermes*, 82 (1954), 300 ff.   [2] Cf. below, p. 89 n. 5.

may be seen in the mad scenes of contemporary comedy of which we know two: in Alexis' *Agonis*, a recognition play produced between 340 and 330, someone feigns madness and parodies the *Orestes*:[1] 'Mother, I beg you, do not brandish Misgolas at me. I am not a citharode.' The other is the mad scene of the *Menaechmi*, which I believe to go back to a comedy of the same date as the *Agonis*; in it we can see reminiscences of the *Bacchae* as well as of the *Iphigenia in Tauris*, *Orestes*, and *Heracles*. Thus the taste for the exciting plays of Euripides evidently continued into the second half of the fourth century, and this agrees with Aristotle's remark that Euripides was the most tragic of poets.[2]

Astydamas, who was victorious in 341 and 340, was a pupil of Isocrates; as also was Aphareus, who won the third prize in 341. Astydamas' *Antigone* (victorious in 341) is probably the source of the story preserved by Hyginus and on an Apulian vase of 330–20 B.C.[3] In this version Haemon had married Antigone and they had a son Maeon; when Antigone buried Polynices, Haemon was ordered to kill her but instead hid her and the baby among shepherds. The play opens when the boy is old enough to come to Thebes for the games and is recognised there by Creon because he has the Spartiate birthmark (the origin of this situation seems to have been Euripides' *Alexandros*). Presumably Creon then ordered Haemon to be put to death. Heracles intervened and begged pardon for Haemon. Heracles' intervention must have been successful (in spite of Hyginus, who has made the story end like Sophocles' *Antigone*). This then seems to have been an exciting play with a happy ending, which further developed the Euripidean version of the Antigone story.

After the production of the *Parthenopaeus* in 340 Astydamas was honoured with a portrait statue in the theatre. For this he composed an inscription, which the Boule rejected.[4] 'Would that I had been born in their day or they in mine, who are thought to

---

[1] Alexis, fr. 3K, cf. *Studies in Later Greek Comedy*, 73.   [2] *Poetics*, 1453 a 29.
[3] Hyginus, *Fab.* lxxii. Apulian vase: Ruvo, Jatta 423. Pickard-Cambridge, *Theatre*, fig. 13.   [4] Photius, 502, 21.

win the prize of a sweet tongue, that I might in truth have been
judged and discharged as superior. But now they are gone ahead
in time where jealousy follows not.' The verses became a proverb
for self-praise, but they also show Astydamas' awareness that the
modern tragedian has a hard battle to establish himself against his
great predecessors. They are a manifesto for modern tragedy
issued a few years before Aristotle and Lycurgus canonised
classical tragedy. What we know about his *Antigone* shows that
Astydamas stood for the long exciting play of varied incident.
His *Alcmaeon* introduced a major variation of the traditional story.
Traditionally, Alcmaeon murdered his mother and was then pur-
sued by Furies. Astydamas made him murder her when he was
mad and later recognise the relationship.[1] We can only suppose
that Alcmaeon was driven mad by his father's command to kill his
mother and killed her in his madness. The new version gave both
a naturalistic mad scene and a terrible recognition afterwards.

In another *Alcmaeon* of this period Theodectes, also a pupil of
Isocrates, made the judges decide that Eriphyle's death was right
but Alcmaeon was wrong to kill her: this is a point of nice discrimination which perhaps belongs rather to the law court than
to the tragic stage. We also know from Aristotle that Theodectes
wrote a *Lynceus*;[2] Hypermnestra unlike her sisters did not murder
her husband, Lynceus, but bore him a son, Abas; the son was
seized and Lynceus condemned to death; then something intervened which caused the death of Danaus and the rescue of
Lynceus. The details are obscure but Aristotle quotes it as an
example of peripety. It is possible that the story was parallel to
the Antigone story discussed above; i.e. that Lynceus is kept
hidden until Abas has grown old enough to come to town for the
games. The story ends with disaster for the villain and success for
the hero, a double plot of the kind which Aristotle says seems to
be the best because of the weakness of the spectators and produces
the pleasure which belongs to comedy rather than to tragedy.

[1] *Poetics*, 1453 b 33, cf. Antiphanes 191 K.
[2] *Poetics*, 1452 a 27; 1455 b 29. Cf. Hyginus, *Fab.* clxx, 9; cclxxiii, 2.

We do not know whether Theodectes' *Mausolus* was about Mausolus of Halicarnassus or about a homonymous ancestor like Euripides' *Archelaus*. It may have been a play of modern history, since it would be more difficult to provide Mausolus than Archelaus with mythical ancestry. Aristotle admits the possibility of historical plays in the *Poetics*,[1] and the most likely explanation of the well-known Apulian vase[2] with Darius and his councillors is that it represents a fourth-century tragedy on the Marathon expedition, written perhaps at the time of Alexander's victories. The figure in the centre standing on a white block labelled *Persai*, wearing *cothurni* and making the gesture that tragic messengers make, seems to me to show that this is a picture inspired by a tragedy. Darius is inscribed, and so the disaster in which the Persian king is involved must be Marathon. He is surrounded by his councillors and his executioner stands behind his chair: two of the councillors are in tragic costume like the king, two in Greek dress, one in Greek dress with a Persian hat; but as the king's treasurer is also in Greek dress, no conclusions can be drawn as to their identity from their costume. Below, the treasurer collects money from representatives of the provinces. Above, Hellas is protected by Zeus and Athena; Asia sits on the altar of Artemis but Artemis has deserted her and Apate with the torches of the Furies is luring her to destruction. The painter has allowed himself great freedom. We may suppose that the play included a description of the royal council (like the description of the assembly in Euripides' *Orestes*) and of the collection of funds, and that the old Aeschylean moral was pointed.

We also know something of two fourth-century plays on the Medea story, which show considerable variations from Euripides. One is by Carcinus, whose name stands first on the fragment of the victor's list. 'In Carcinus' *Medea*', according to Aristotle,[3] 'they accuse her of killing the children as they cannot be found

---

[1] *Poetics*, 1451 b 29.   [2] Naples 3253. Pickard-Cambridge, *Festivals*, fig. 191.
[3] *Rhetoric*, 1400 b 9. The *Medea* preserved by a papyrus fragment (Milne, *Catalogue*, no. 77) is too fragmentary for reconstruction.

D

anywhere. Medea made a mistake in sending the children away. She answers that she would not have killed the children but Jason: for it would have been a mistake to omit to kill Jason if she had killed the children.' This version differs considerably from Euripides, and Medea's self-defence that it would have been a mistake to omit to kill Jason if she had killed the children is a direct criticism of Euripides. It sounds as if she somehow sent the children away before she murdered Jason's new wife and then was accused by Creon and Jason (?) of also murdering her own children. We can at least say that Carcinus was an original tragedian who introduced variations into the great fifth-century version of the legend and was perhaps less tied to Euripides than his earlier contemporaries.

We have a picture of the other *Medea*, which was at any rate acted in the fourth century, on an Apulian vase of 330–300.[1] As in Euripides, the princess is poisoned and Creon is involved in her disaster, but her mother Merope and her brother Hippotes come to her help and it seems unlikely that the painter invented them. Medea slays one child but a young man hurries away with another (Diodorus has a version in which one of three children was saved); here again it is impossible that the painter should insert this incident if he was illustrating a performance of Euripides' play. The ghost of Aetes (Medea's father) stands on a rock and surveys the scene in horror; he again can hardly be the painter's invention. Finally, Oistros (madness) is shown in a snaky chariot. Here then we have another version closely dependent on Euripides, but embroidering the death of the princess and altering the murder of the children, introducing also the spectacular figures of Madness and the Ghost of Aetes.

A play of a different character was Chairemon's *Achilles Thersitoctonus*, which was produced before 350, as is proved by dated quotations[2] of a famous line: 'human life is chance, not forethought.' The play is illustrated on an Apulian vase of about

---

[1] Munich 810 (J). Pickard-Cambridge, *Theatre*, fig. 21; *Greek Theatre Production*, no. A42.   [2] e.g. Plato, *Laws*, 709b.

330 B.C.[1] The brief summary of the Cyclic epic *Aethiopis* tells us that after the burial of Penthesilea 'Achilles kills Thersites, having been abused by him and taunted with his alleged love for Penthesilea. The Achaeans then quarrelled about the death of Thersites. After this Achilles sailed to Lesbos and having sacrificed to Apollo, Artemis, and Leto was purified by Odysseus.' These are the bare bones of the tragedy. The vase shows us centrally Achilles springing up, I think, from his couch in spite of the protestations of his elderly friend, Phoenix, and below, the body and severed head of Thersites lying among a collection of overturned and broken pots and pans, watched by Automedon, the charioteer of Achilles; a slave runs away presumably to tell the news. On the right Diomede, the cousin of Thersites, rushes up with an Aetolian soldier to avenge him but is restrained by Menelaus; on the left Agamemnon approaches with Phorbas, and above Poina broods over the scene. This was evidently a play of camp life like the *Rhesus* and the rough-house reminds us of Demosthenes' description of camp life in his *Conon*. Agamemnon presumably settled the quarrel between Achilles and Diomede, and Achilles agreed to go to Lesbos for purification. Poina is perhaps both the vengeance that Achilles exacts from Thersites and the vengeance that Diomede wishes to exact from Achilles.

If we put together what we know of the practice of fourth-century tragedy with the theory of the *Poetics*, the *Poetics* becomes easier to appreciate. In practice the long and exciting play with hairbreadth escapes, violent incidents, and sometimes nice discrimination of motives held the stage. We can understand that such plays kept the audience in emotional tension. We cannot know anything of their composition from the fragments, but Theodectes' *Lynceus* is quoted by Aristotle beside the *Oedipus Tyrannus*, and Theodectes, Astydamas, and Aphareus were all pupils of Isocrates, whose concern with composition has been illustrated. This kind of tragedy Aristotle could justify morally and politically by the theory of *katharsis*; its organic structure

[1] Here, Pl. 9. Boston, 03.804. Beazley, *AJA*, 54 (1950), 322.

agreed with his own view of Nature, which Art copied. He added his own conception of universality, and so formulated his view of the tragic hero (the man who falls from high estate and prosperity because of a *hamartia*), the other characters (their colour must be good, etc.), the tragic deed (performed on a kinsman with or without knowledge), the tragic scene (peripety and recognition), and the speeches (calculated to have the maximum effect on the audience). Tragedy is a kind of rhetoric designed to arouse certain emotions. The concept of *hamartia*, which is fundamental for the tragic hero, and the concept of Ignorance, which is fundamental for the tragic deed, are discussed in Aristotle's *Ethics*, but the question there also is connected with justice and the courts. You judge a man differently if he has acted in ignorance or without premeditation or with premeditation. These distinctions not only define the deed but also determine the jury's reaction to the doer. So in the *Poetics* Aristotle chooses this particular kind of hero and this particular kind of deed because he wants a particular reaction (pity and fear) in the audience.

We agree with much that he says as eminently sensible and yet he seems to have left out much that moves us most in Greek tragedy. The poetry of the choruses, the moral stature of Antigone or Oedipus, the comment which relates them to the divine government of the world and so to us, these may serve as symbols of what we find most valuable in Greek tragedy. We cannot say for certain that they had faded from fourth-century tragedy, but Aristotle's statement that interludes which could be transferred from play to play were the normal rule in fourth-century tragedy is confirmed by papyrus fragments. With the choruses goes to a large extent the poet's opportunity to comment on his story and to relate it to universal laws, which are valid for all human affairs and not only for the very special sequence of events constituting a Greek tragedy. Aristotle sees this when he says that the chorus should be treated as one of the actors.[1] The other form of comment which the poet makes is to show us people of great moral

[1] *Poetics*, 1456 a 25.

stature; here again there are two hints[1] that Aristotle found this in classical tragedy but not in contemporary tragedy. One is the passage where he misses the quality of *ethos*—here something like 'moral purpose', as is shown by his comparison with the art of Zeuxis and Polygnotus—and the other where he contrasts the rhetorical speeches of modern tragedy with the statesmanlike speeches of earlier tragedy (this view too was surely formed in his early years in Athens). But these are three isolated hints which are not developed. In fact the *Poetics* gives us two things which are not quite compatible; admiration of classical tragedy on every page but standards of criticism formed in the rhetorical school, obedience to which could never produce an *Oedipus* or *Antigone* but might produce intensely moving tragi-comedy.

4. COMEDY

The *Poetics* did in fact influence the comedy of Menander but that comes later. Yet the *Poetics* itself shows that Middle Comedy had by the thirties developed in the direction of New Comedy. When Aristotle[2] argues that poetry is more philosophical than history because it aims at the universal, he defines universality by saying that 'a man of a certain kind probably or necessarily speaks or acts in a certain way . . . this is now clear in the case of comedy because the poets construct the plots of probable incidents and then add chance names'. We must therefore assume that by the time Aristotle wrote the *Poetics* there was a comedy with clearly marked imaginary characters and incidents following each other in a probable sequence as in tragedy. What evidence have we for this development? In the first place, we have noticed political criticism in comedy and we can quote instances of political characters being brought on the stage. Aristotle's statement about chance names must therefore be accepted with reservation.

It is equally clear that mythological characters are formally

[1] *Poetics*, 1450 a 25, b 7.   [2] *Poetics*, 1451 b 11.

excluded, and yet the *Poetics*[1] quotes a comedy in which 'Orestes and Aegisthus go off as friends at the end and nobody is killed by anybody'. But the decline of mythological comedy during our period is remarkable. In the first half of the fourth century something between a third and a half of the dated plays have mythological titles, but between 350 and 320 the proportion falls to a tenth. This strongly suggests that the desire for probable incidents and chance names gradually killed the old type of mythological comedy, however strongly the new type of comedy was itself influenced by tragedy in choice of situations. But the fragments of mythological comedy show that the old formula continued in use: the tragic story is transferred to the lowest level of contemporary life. Eubulus' *Dolon*[2] is so fat that he cannot tie his shoes up, and he has never had to wash up because he always licks the plates clean. Eubulus' *Auge* is probably illustrated by a set of mid-fourth-century terracottas found in a grave in Athens and by a Campanian vase of the third quarter of the fourth century.[3] Heracles is a fat, goggling-eyed monster and the other characters are indistinguishable from the normal actors of Old and Middle Comedy with padding, phallus, and grotesque masks. Significantly, the one late mythological comedy which we possess is much less earthy. The original of Plautus' *Amphitruo* was probably produced in the early twenties of the fourth century. Hermes behaves like a comic slave and Zeus has a touch of the braggart soldier, but this is much milder caricature of divine and heroic life than we expect in Middle Comedy. Alcmene retains so much of her tragic colouring that it is not a long step from her to Pamphile in Menander's *Epitrepontes*; here parody of tragedy fades into Comedy of Manners.

Even for the characters of comedy who are neither mythological

---

[1] *Poetics*, 1453 a 36. Cf. *Studies in Later Greek Comedy*, 85 f.   [2] fr. 30K.
[3] Terracottas: the set is in New York, 13.225.14 ff., Pickard-Cambridge, *Festivals*, figs. 84–8; Bieber, *HT*, figs. 122 ff. Campanian vase: Leontini. Bieber, *HT*, fig. 358; Beazley, *JHS*, 63 (1943), 107; *Greek Theatre Production*, nos. B11, 67.

nor political Aristotle's statement needs some annotation.[1] It is certainly true that stock characters develop during this period and that they belong to a stratum of upper-class Athenian life much concerned with feasting and love-making. The characters are however sometimes given real names rather than chance names. Thus living *hetairai* had been put on the stage before 370 and the practice continued; but the names of real *hetairai* were also used for imaginary *hetairai*, and not only for rich and grasping *hetairai* but also for young girls, who are the heroines of the new intrigue comedy. The braggart soldier started as a historical character with Lamachus in the *Acharnians* and in the fourth century Philip of Macedon was the braggart soldier in a comedy by Mnesimachus, but three plays in this period are simply called *Soldier* and it is a reasonable assumption that their heroes were imaginary and had chance names. Similarly we know both historical and chance names for parasites and cooks. Thus the interweaving of historical reality and fiction both in giving names and, we may assume, in actually drawing the characters was much more subtle than Aristotle's brief formulation suggests. On the other hand such titles as *Soldier, Rustic, Brothelkeeper, Hermit, Pot-Belly, Busybody* show that characters of clear and distinctive types had been developed and presumably the plots of these plays displayed their particular characteristics and were determined by them.

In the fragments we can see traces of plots which look forward to the intrigue and recognition plays of Menander and his contemporaries. One of the more interesting is Eubulus' *Stephanopolides*,[2] because it shows elements of both old and new. A *hetaira* does not want her daughter to fall hopelessly in love; if she goes on living (marriage is death) she will be more profitable to her mother. The garland-sellers form the chorus and enter singing about their garlands and the *hetairai* who might wear them. They try to sell their garlands to the *hetaira* and her daughter, who evidently want to beat down their prices; the leader of the

[1] Cf. *Studies in Later Greek Comedy*, 63 ff.
[2] Cf. *Studies in Later Greek Comedy*, 61.

garland-sellers says that at least she and her friends do not use excessive make-up like the prostitutes. There is also a lover, who is accused of being excessively timorous and has a rich rival. Here we have on the one hand a named chorus—the garland-sellers—singing a special entrance song about living *hetairai* and taking part in the dialogue as in Aristophanes, and on the other hand characters typical of New Comedy—*hetaira*, girl, lover, rival, slave.

Such a cast appears on a relief celebrating the production of a comedy in the Attic deme of Aixone almost certainly in the year 340–339 B.C.[1] Five masks have been carved along a bar above the inscription: a bearded old man, an oldish woman with straggly unkempt hair and longish nose, a slave, a youth with raised brows and wild hair, and a girl with short hair tied in some sort of knot at the bottom. It is a reasonable guess that the young man is in love with the girl and that the slave in the middle intrigues to help him. The old pair may be father of the youth and mother of the girl but other combinations are conceivable. There is apparently no mask for the chorus; presumably therefore, as in New Comedy, the chorus only sang interludes and took no part in the dialogue.

For plays as a whole we only have the *Menaechmi* and *Persa* of Plautus, of which the Greek originals can be dated in the neighbourhood of 340.[2] We have already noticed that the mad scene of the *Menaechmi* parodies the mad scenes of Euripidean tragedy; in the *Persa* the girl, who is dressed up as an Arabian captive, speaks a string of high moral sentiments, neatly rounded and ultimately derived from Greek tragedy. Otherwise, if we grant the initial improbability of the twins in the *Menaechmi* wearing identical clothes, these plays conform to the Aristotelian definition: given people of this type (greedy *hetaira*, stupid wife in the *Menaechmi*, hungry parasite, ingenious slave, and shameless brothelkeeper in the *Persa*) these sorts of things will happen to

---

[1] Pickard-Cambridge, *Festivals*, fig. 18; Webster, *JHS*, 71 (1951), 222, n. 7; *Studies in Later Greek Comedy*, pl. III; *Greek Theatre Production*, no. B31.

[2] Cf. *Studies in Later Greek Comedy*, 70, 78.

them. There is no moral, and the characterisation though clear is superficial, but the plots are well constructed and can today be played to uproarious laughter, which was their object.

We cannot gain an entirely clear picture of comedy because our evidence is fragmentary and in all probability comedy did not itself have a uniform style. We know the end of the development in the character comedy of Menander and his contemporaries, but in Middle Comedy both the plots and the characters were being created, developed, or borrowed. In the *Persa* the plot is much more important than the characters: the absurd intrigue is an end in itself and not, as later, a piece of machinery for setting the characters in motion. The characters must often have been caricatures rather than characters, and sometimes they were satirical portraits of contemporaries in the old manner. Naturalism was hampered by the grotesque masks and obscene costume. Yet these poets achieved the creation of character types which later poets could individualise—mean and angry father, lovesick or extravagant son, clever slave, braggart soldier, greedy *hetaira*, virtuous *hetaira*. And they achieved this while maintaining much that was traditional in comedy such as the occasional extravagant phantasy of the old type, the earthy parodies of tragic themes, and the criticism of politicians and philosophers.

5. PROSE STYLE

For tragedy and comedy we have enough evidence to show that to stir the emotions of the audience by organic composition was not only theory but practice. Later we shall have to consider art and portraiture, but first we may consider briefly from this point of view theory and practice in prose style, since Aristotle frequently refers to rhetoric in the *Poetics* and the tragic poet Theodectes was famous also as a rhetorician. On the large scale of the speech Isocrates seems to have thought of composition in terms of its effect on the audience, and Theodectes defined the different emotional effects which different parts of the speech

should have. Today it is difficult to conceive that the surviving
works of Isocrates could have stirred emotion, and we should
probably not describe the longer sentences which occur in them,
however rhythmical and however often divided and subdivided,
as organic composition. But the speeches of Lycurgus and
Dinarchus show a yet more ponderous, long-winded, and complicated version of what is essentially the same style and therefore
we must suppose that it had a practical efficacy which escapes us.

On the other hand we see in Demosthenes a style which we can
readily define as organic composition for emotional effect. His
sentences show a very high degree of organisation both by sub-
ordination of clauses and by subdivision. It is possible to see
certain principles which guided him. The structure of the sentence
must be clear, and therefore the main sentence, the foundation on
which the whole period is built, must be kept in view; the dependent clauses are built into the fabric of the main sentence, or, if
they are appended at the end, careful preparation is made for them
earlier in the sentence. The famous narrative in the *Crown* in
which Demosthenes[1] describes the capture of Elateia leads up to
the climax where Demosthenes comes forward in the assembly
and makes his speech. It starts with a double sentence: 'It was
evening and a man came with a message for the prytanies that
Elateia had been captured.' Then two longish periods describe
the confusion in the city and the assembling of the Council and
Ecclesia; each ends with a short member 'confusion filled the city',
'all the people were seated above'. Then a period introduced by a
long tripartite temporal clause ends with a double sentence 'the
herald asked "Who wishes to speak?" but none came forward'.
Then a period which has triple concessive participial clauses with
anaphora explains that no one spoke although everybody was
there. Then a long period argues that the time needed neither
good will nor money but knowledge of Philip's career and plans:
it is a double period with the first part again subdivided into three
sentences introduced by conditional clauses and the second part

[1] Demosthenes, xviii, 169.

also subdivided and followed by a 'for' sentence which gives its opposite. Then the climax: 'I then stood forth on that day as this man.' Demosthenes uses on the whole larger elements than Plato or Lysias, and works not only with parallelism of corresponsive participles and loose correspondence of structure but also with the contrast of short and long members at the end of periods and at the end of the whole passage. The story is brilliantly composed to produce the excitement and suspense which Demosthenes needs before describing his own policy. This is undoubtedly organic composition directed at the emotions of the audience.

The theory is found, as we have already noted, in the *Phaedrus* and reappears in Aristotle's *Rhetoric*. Much of the second book and some of the first is concerned with the problem of adapting the speech to the minds of the audience (whether an audience of listeners or of readers) by producing in them the emotions that the orator desires, thus creating the desired attitude to himself (or his client) and to his adversary. What Aristotle has to say about composition is found in the later chapters of the third book, which are reasonably supposed to be particularly close to Theodectes. He again uses the metaphor of a body with a head,[1] which Plato had used in the *Phaedrus* and which Aristotle elaborates further in the *Poetics*.

From our particular point of view the most interesting passage is the discussion of periodic sentences in the ninth chapter. At the end Aristotle refers to Theodectes: 'the principles (or virtues) of periods are enumerated in the Theodectea.'[2] This appears to mean that the chief things to be aimed at in writing periods were enumerated by Theodectes in his *Art* and have been included by Aristotle in his précis of it. It is noticeable that in discussing the period with members Aristotle gives no less than nine examples from Isocrates' *Panegyricus*, and we may therefore assume that the principles (or virtues) established by Theodectes concerned the period with members. But we have no reason to attribute

---

[1] *Rhetoric*, 1415 b 8. On the relation of iii, 13–19 with Theodectes, see F. Solmsen, *Hermes*, 67 (1932), 147 f.   [2] *Rhetoric*, 1410 b 2.

either the essential distinction between the 'strung together' style
(*eiromene*) and 'the knotted' (*katestrammene*) style or the theory
of the period to anyone but Aristotle. The only unity in the
eiromene is the unity given by connecting particles. It has no other
end than the end of the subject-matter. Aristotle dislikes this style
because it has no bounds. It is impossible to foresee the end. To
foresee the end some other unity is needed than that given by connecting particles. This criterion justifies us in including in Aristotle's *eiromene* much early narrative, which consists of simple
sentences connected by 'and' and 'but', and scientific descriptions
such as are found for instance in Theophrastus' *History of Plants*.

Aristotle defines a period as having 'a beginning and end of its
own and a length which can be seen at one time. It is pleasing
because the hearer thinks that he has something and that something has been concluded for him. To foresee nothing and to
complete nothing is unpleasant. It is easy to learn because it has
number.' This account of the period reproduces in miniature his
account of composition in the *Poetics*: it must have organic construction and it must be of the right size to be comprehensible.
The parts of the period can be numbered off so that like verse it
is easy to remember; primarily this means, no doubt, that any part
introduced by a corresponsive particle demands its response, but
perhaps Aristotle is also thinking of adverbial expressions which
point forward to a following final, causal or other clause and on
the other hand of clauses which point forward to a coming main
sentence. The period has signposts; they are easy to remember
and they mark ground gained.

Aristotle then divides periods into periods with members and
smooth periods, and further subdivides periods with members into
'divided' and 'antithetic', and adds further characteristics 'equality
of length of members' and 'similarity of beginning and ending of
members'. It is clear that by 'members' Aristotle means primarily
the pairs of sentences, clauses, phrases, and words connected
normally by corresponsive particles, which we have noticed as
distinctive of Isocrates and his successors. Aristotle himself gives

illustrations from Isocrates' *Panegyricus* and at the end of the section comes the reference to Theodectes. It seems certain that the technical terms *parisosis, parhomoiosis*, etc. were used by Theodectes if they were not actually invented by him. Theodectes was a pupil of Isocrates and presumably liked this kind of prose; how Aristotle, with his admirably sensible views on sentence construction and his fine, nervous style, could endure the endless sentences of Isocrates is hard to understand. We must assume that he perceived its effect on the insensitive and solaced himself with counting corresponsive particles. However that may be, we must also remember that the Aristotelian syllogism in its correct form ('if A is predicated of all B, and B is predicated of all C, it is necessary that A should be predicated of all C')[1] is a period with members.

Aristotle has only given us a summary theory of sentence-construction and we have no right to press him too far. He has fastened on three essential points, the aimlessness of the 'strung-along style', the sense of organisation given by pairing, and the essential quality of the period—to be a comprehensible organic construction. The remaining question is what he meant by the smooth period. He defines it as *monokolos*. I find this difficult to understand in the sense of 'with a single member', since a line must be drawn between the 'smooth period' and 'the strung-along style'. In the *Parts of animals*[2] *monokotylos* means not 'with a single sucker' but 'with a single row of suckers' as distinct from 'with a double row of suckers'. It is clear that the essential feature of the period with members according to Aristotle is pairing. It seems therefore possible that *monokolos* means 'with a single row of members' as distinct from 'with paired members'. The smooth period is then not unlike the 'simple tragedy', which has a straight progression from happiness to misfortune. In this kind of period the organic structure is particularly clear. The organisation con-

---

[1] *An. Pr.* i, 4, 25 b 37. Cf. J. Lukasiewicz, *Aristotle's Syllogistic*, 3.

[2] *de part. An.* 685 b 11, Quintilian, ix, 4, 124, seems to have misunderstood this. Dion. Hal. *de Dem.* 2 on Lysias' smooth style.

sists of clauses and participial phrases grouped round a main sentence so that the conditions determining or determined by the proposition made in the main sentence are stated in their proper relationship to it. Some slight support to this interpretation is given by Dionysius' use of 'smooth' to characterise the style of Lysias; Lysias, as we have seen, is the orator in whom this particular form of sentence construction is most obvious. Thus, although Aristotle's sketch of sentence construction is so brief and although the existence of Theodectes' enumeration of Isocratean virtues in period construction has led him to overemphasise the period constructed of paired members, it is possible to claim his advocacy for the nervous athletic prose which is spare and moving in Lysias, slightly fleshier but very effective in Demosthenes, and reduced to its essentials in Aristotle's own treatises.[1]

6. ART

We have said something already of official art as well as of art in the service of tragedy and comedy. Official art provides a useful starting-point also for considering the nature of painting and sculpture during this period and their relation to the philosophers. Two comments are preserved on Euphranor's pictures, which were painted after the battle of Mantinea in 362: the battle picture showed according to Plutarch[2] the clash and strain of battle, full of strength and wrath and spirit, and the Theseus according to the artist himself[3] was 'fed on beef' while the Theseus of Parrhasius, the painter of the late fifth century, had been fed on 'roses'. It appears that Euphranor, whose career lasted at least from 365 to 340, broke away from the rich style of his predecessors with their slim, youthful figures of gods and heroes. His

---

[1] Cf. I. Düring, *Lychnos*, 1943, 58 f. for a comparison of Aristotle's theory and practice.

[2] Plutarch, *de Gloria Atheniensium*, 2 (Overbeck, 1795).

[3] Pliny, *NH*, xxxv, 129 (Overbeck, 1790).

heroes had dignity (the Greek is probably *semnotes*). This was partly due to their musculature (Theseus is fed on beef), and partly because deformities such as Hephaestus' lameness are suppressed. Violent action is not excluded as Plutarch's description of the battle-picture shows. The Twelve Gods and the Theseus showed gods and hero at peace, and the battle showed modern heroes in action. We may remember what Plato[1] said about the need for both the courageous heart and the modest spirit in the state, and the dignity of Euphranor's heroes may be regarded as an answer to Plato's criticisms in the *Republic*. We cannot name any certain copy or even reflection of Euphranor's work, but we can imagine its quality from contemporary Athenian vases.

I suggested in the last chapter that the gods who look on at ease while mortals struggle and the gods who are young and slim and beautiful were an artistic expression of the bliss, agelessness, and detachment ascribed to the divine by the philosophers. The effortless divine onlooker is rarer now, and perhaps only Praxiteles continues the tradition of the detached young god, the young satyr idealised so that practically nothing of the boisterous, wanton man of the woods remains, or Hermes abstractedly dangling a bunch of grapes in front of the infant Dionysus, or Aphrodite with her 'secret haughty smile'[2] as she prepares to take her bath. If we want to imagine Euphranor's Twelve Gods, we must not think of them in terms of Praxiteles but rather of the assemblies of gods on Kertch vases. On one of 360–50 in the British Museum[3] Heracles and the Dioscuri arrive in Eleusis by night to be initiated by Demeter and Kore, who are attended by Eumolpus, Iacchus,

---

[1] *Politicus*, 306, cf. also the two kinds of music in *Rep.*, 399 a–c.

[2] Richter, figs. 682–4; 664–5, 668–72. Lucian, *Amores*, 13 (Overbeck, 1234).

[3] British Museum, F68. Here Pl. 10*a*. Metzger, 245/13 (and 126/36); Schefold, *U.*, no. 94. Cf. assemblies of Eleusinian deities on Tübingen, E183 (Metzger, 244/12; Schefold, *U.*, no. 46) and Istanbul (Metzger, 245/14; Schefold, *U.*, no. 152) and epiphanies of Aphrodite on Dresden, ZV. 1517 (Metzger, 68/13; Schefold, *U.*, no. 64) and Salonika (Metzger, 70/14; Schefold, *U.*, no. 564a; *Olynthus*, v, 123 f.).

and Triptolemus, five tremendous figures filling the centre of the picture. A similar scene later (340–30)[1] shows Demeter seated in the centre with Triptolemus in his winged chariot above her head and the child Plutus standing at her right side, to the right Kore standing, Dionysus and Themis (seated) and to the left Aphrodite seated with a tiny Eros at her feet and Iacchus and Heracles standing; here we can truly see Euphranor's *dignitates heroum*. Three points distinguish the pictures of the third quarter of the century from their predecessors: a high proportion of the figures are frontal (as also on contemporary grave-reliefs) and so in direct communication with the spectator; they are of great size in proportion to the frame (this is the *megethos* lauded by Aristotle in the *Poetics*); and the deep setting of the eyes gives them a sombre passion quite different from the sunny detachment of Praxitelean heads.

This solemn Demeter reminds us of the contemporary Demeter of Cnidus,[2] which has recently been attributed to the Athenian sculptor Leochares. A wonderful Apollo in the Marsyas scene on another Kertch vase has been said to derive from a sculptural original by Euphranor or Scopas.[3] We have already spoken of Euphranor; the deep setting of the eyes is characteristic of the Parian sculptor Scopas, who carved an Apollo Citharoedus for Rhamnus in Attica.[4] He also carved a great group of Poseidon, Thetis, Achilles, Nereids riding sea monsters, Tritons, and other sea beasts, which is known in many reflections and presumably inspired the group in the sanctuary of Poseidon at Atlantis described by Plato.[5] His Maenad moves in abandoned ecstasy, a

---

[1] Leningrad, St. 1792; Metzger, 244/11; Schefold, *U.*, no. 368. Cf. Oxford, Al Mina 86, Metzger, 162/20; Beazley, *JHS*, 59 (1939), 35. Contrast the later hydria in Lyons, Metzger, 293/10; Schefold, *U.*, no. 187; Pickard-Cambridge, *Festivals*, fig. 163.

[2] Richter, fig. 315. Cf. B. Ashmole, *JHS*, 71 (1951), 13 f.

[3] Leningrad, St. 1795. Metzger, 162/18; Schefold, *U.*, no. 370. On sculptural source see Schefold, *op. cit.*, 128; Picard, *IVe*, 864.

[4] Pliny, *NH*, xxxvi, 25 (Overbeck, 1159).

[5] Pliny, *NH*, xxxvi, 26 (Overbeck, 1175). Cf. Metzger, 293; Rumpf, *Meerwesen*, 117. Plato, *Critias*, 116d.

sculptured parallel to the ecstatic Dionysiac scenes on contemporary vases.[1] Scopas is the sculptor of passionate movement. At Tegea, where he designed the sculpture, one pediment had the Calydonian boar hunt and the other the battle between Telephus and Achilles as subject. Scopas also, if the tradition is true, was in charge of the east side of the Mausoleum. The fierce Amazonomachies of the Mausoleum frieze are paralleled by many Attic vases where the combatants are sometimes Greeks, sometimes Greeks and Orientals (whether Amazons or Persians is often difficult to distinguish),[2] and sometimes Arimaspians and Griffins.[3] We need not search for any symbolism here beyond the obvious equation of the mythical battles with contemporary battles; like Euphranor's Battle of Mantinea these mythical combats evoke 'the manly heart'.

Euphranor contrasted his beef-fed Theseus with Parrhasius' rose-fed Theseus. Two pictures of Heracles in the garden of the Hesperides, one from the late fifth century and one from the second quarter of the fourth century,[4] show the contrast between the Rose-fed and the Beef-fed hero. The later picture is an admirably clean composition centred on Heracles. This kind of composition came in with the transition from the rich style to the Kertch style of vase-painting.

I quote as a very fine instance a pelike in Leningrad[5] with the Calydonian boar hunt. The boar is central with Ancaeus above him and Artemis in the background; the hunters are concentrated on the boar, and there are two other points of interest, Atalanta

[1] Richter, fig. 709. Vases: e.g. Leningrad, St. 2007 (Metzger, 107/5; Schefold, U., no. 18); Leningrad, Inv. 6791 (Schefold, U., no. 364); Leningrad, St. 1788 (Metzger, 131/48; Schefold, U., no. 366).

[2] e.g. British Museum, E233 (Metzger, 329/56; Schefold, U., no. 176); Leningrad, 26.1.1913/8 (Schefold, U., no. 1).

[3] e.g. British Museum, E434. Metzger, 328/51; Schefold, U., no. 513; Pfuhl, MuZ, fig. 602.

[4] British Museum, E224. Cf. above, Ch. I, p. 14 n. 2 (cf. here Pl. 7 by the same painter). E227. Here Pl. 10b; Metzger, 202/19; Schefold, U., no. 170; Rumpf, MuZ, 133.

[5] Here Pl. 11. Leningrad, B4528. Metzger, 313/26; Schefold, U., no. 483.

with her bow on the extreme left and Thersites (?) surveying the scene with horror on the extreme right. In such clean drawing and clear composition it is natural to see the influence of the Sicyonian painter Pamphilus, who was especially skilled in arithmetic and geometry and succeeded in having drawing included as a fourth liberal art in all the schools of Sicyon and then of the rest of Greece.[1] We can follow the tradition in Athenian vase-painting. An admirable example is the Dionysus and Ariadne in London:[2] a central group of four, seated maenad, little white Eros, seated Dionysus and Ariadne, is flanked on the left by a young satyr standing and a little scrubby Pan running away and on the right by a standing maenad, a seated Pan with a harp, and a little veiled Night. We know also that the Sicyonian painter Melanthius, who was the pupil of Pamphilus, was acknowledged by Apelles as his master in composition, and we have a superb composition in the mosaic of the battle of Darius and Alexander[3] copied from a painting of about 330. Although the treatment of the ground as a flat stage is helpless, the skill with which Alexander and the Persian king are made to stand out from the massed figures, the use of slanting spears to give depth and back boundary and of the foreshortened horse to give depth from in front is masterly. The practice of the artists corresponds with the theory of the philosophers that composition is an element of beauty.[4]

The emotions of the spectator are stirred sometimes by the frontality of the figures, sometimes by their size in their frames, sometimes by their violence or passion, sometimes by their

---

[1] Pliny, *NH*, xxxv, 76 (Overbeck, 1748). P. was possibly in Athens before 388. Cf. Ar. *Plut.* 385 and scholia.

[2] British Museum, E228. Metzger, 120/30; Schefold, *U.*, no. 171. Cf. the following, in chronological order: (*a*) Ge and Plutus (?), Istanbul (Metzger, 244/12; Schefold, *U.*, no. 152). (*b*) Adonis festival, British Museum, E241 (Metzger, 93/43; Schefold, *U.*, no. 181). (*c*) Apollo and Marsyas, cf. above, p. 80 n. 3.

[3] Here Pl. 12. Naples, NM 10020. Pfuhl, *MuZ*, fig. 648; Beazley and Ashmole, *Gr. Sculpt. and Painting*, fig. 142; Rumpf, *JHS*, 67 (1947), 15 f.; *MuZ*, 148; von Salis, *Antike und Renaissance*, 89 f.

[4] e.g. Plato, *Laws*, 668; Aristotle, *Poetics*, 1450 b 37; *Metaphysics*, 1078 a 36.

realistic representation, which awakes our sympathy. The foreshortened horse in the mosaic rendered by modelling its hind-
quarters in colour ranging from deepest black to brightest white
is a remarkable achievement of realistic technique like the reflection of the Persian's face in the shield, which can be seen to the
right of the horse. The latter reminds us of the picture of Methe
by Pausias, another pupil of Pamphilus: 'you can see in the picture', says Pausanias,[1] 'a glass cup and through it the woman's
face.' Pausias also painted a foreshortened ox, in which he achieved
a great effect of depth without highlights by modelling in different
tones of black. He was the first expert in the comparatively new
technique of encaustic, the ancient equivalent of oils, and, perhaps
to discover the full possibilities of his technique, painted small
pictures of boys and of flowers.[2] A reflection of his art can be seen
in the extremely beautiful flowers and scrolls on Apulian vases of
the second half of the fourth century and in the still life of masks,
tables, mixing bowls, musical instruments, hares, and birds on the
South Italian vases with decoration in added colour which are
known as Gnathia vases; similarly the very careful perspective
drawing of a palace on a Gnathia vase of the mid-fourth century
was connected by Bulle with the draughtsmanship of Pamphilus,
Pausias' teacher.[3] Attic vases occasionally have effective architectural backgrounds; rocks are regularly drawn with shaded
folds of stone and sometimes a hollow beneath, and grasses and
flowers are indicated upon them. On two vases a much more
elaborate cave is outlined in white stone, the inside is red with
receding patches of black, and plenty of plant life is visible both

---

[1] Pausanias, ii, 27, 3 (Overbeck, 1761). Cf. below, p. 105.

[2] Pliny, *NH*, xxxv, 123–7 (Overbeck, 1760). Cf. also the floral border to a
painting of Apelles, Webster, *JJP*, 5 (1951) on Roberts, *JJP*, 4 (1950), 215.

[3] The link between Apulian florals (of which a good collection is given in
Annali, 1843, pl. O, cf. also here Pl. 9) and Peloponnesian art is given by a pebble
mosaic in Epidaurus (Rumpf, *MuZ*, 139, fig. 16). On repertoire of Gnathia see
Rocco, *Memorie della Accademia di Napoli*, 6 (1940), 11. The Gnathia palace:
Pickard-Cambridge, *Theatre*, figs. 55–6; Bulle, *eine Skenographie*, 23; *Greek Theatre
Production*, no. A35.

outside and in.[1] A Corinthian mirror[2] brings us back to the neighbourhood of Pausias, who came from Sicyon: a nymph is washing her hair in a cave while a Pan looks on. The tunnel of the cave surrounds the whole picture; it is silvered and only a few stones are left in the darker bronze; wreaths and fillets are hung in the entrance and plants grow from the floor.

The Athenian painter Nicias, who was painting from the middle of the century onwards, said that the painter should not carve up his art into small subjects such as birds and flowers, and this is naturally supposed to be a criticism of Pausias; if Pompeian copies of his own pictures are to be trusted, the landscape elements are vague in the extreme and correspond to Plato's remark in the *Critias*[3] that 'we have quite a different standard for judging paintings of the human body and paintings of landscape; for the latter in our absence of knowledge we are satisfied with illusionistic shading'. Aristotle[4] would not have been so critical of small subjects, since he noted as evidence for delight in *mimesis* our joy in accurate pictures of minor animals and dead bodies, which give us the reverse of pleasure when seen in actuality. Our pleasure is due to the skill of the artist, and we may remember not only the birds of Pausias, but also the birds and hares of Gnathia vases, and the charming pictures of fish on Attic and South Italian vases.[5] When Aristotle mentioned dead bodies he may have been think-

---

[1] Architecture: British Museum, F68 (cf. above, p. 79 n. 3); Munich, 2398, Schefold, *U.*, no. 103. Landscape: British Museum, 1901.7.10.5, Metzger, 111/8; Schefold, *U.*, no. 515. Leningrad, St. 1788, cf. above, p. 81 n. 1. Amsterdam, 3505, Metzger, 203/22; Schefold, *U.*, no. 355. Caves: Berlin, F2646, Metzger, 75/17; Powell, *New Chapters*[3], 90, fig. 3. Leningrad, St. 1792, cf. above, p. 80 n. 1.

[2] Here Pl. 13*b*. Berlin, 8148: Zuchner, *Klappspiegel*, no. 59; Pfuhl, *MuZ*, fig. 625.

[3] Demetrius, *On Style*, 76 (Overbeck, 1825); Pfuhl, *MuZ*, figs. 646–7; Rumpf, *MuZ*, pl. 47, 1–2. Plato, *Critias*, 107b.

[4] *Poetics*, 1448 b 11, cf. *de part. An.* 645 a 11.

[5] Fishplates: Lacroix, *Faune marine*; Schefold, *U.*, nos. 47–59; Robinson, *Olynthus*, xiii, 124; Aurigemma, *Museo di Spina*, 148. Rumpf compares pebble mosaic in Olympia, *MuZ*, 123.

ing of Silanion's dying Iocasta, for which the sculptor used a special admixture of silver for the face 'that the bronze might make it clear that she was wasting away and dying'.[1] Another example is the group of Niobe watching her sons and daughters fall beneath the arrows of Apollo and Artemis.[2]

Such works prompt the question how far realism is compatible with 'the dignity of heroes'. The answer may be that 'dignity' was preserved by the large scale of the figures in relation to their frame and that the spectator was carried away by the emotion. Nicias himself demanded heroic subjects because he thought that the subject stood in the same relation to painting as the plot to the drama. But this view, which must surely have arisen from a know-ledge of Aristotle, did not prohibit realistic treatment. His Andromeda, according to an epigram, dragged her feet sluggishly from the rock after the long torture. If we can trust the Pompeian copy, the emphasis was on the central figure of Andromeda slowly descending, as if she was scarcely yet aware that she was safe and free, much less that Perseus loved her. Further, if the relation to the frame is correctly preserved in the best copy, she appears as a tremendous figure and the spectator, like Perseus, is swept into sympathy. The formula, organic composition directed at the emotions of the audience, can usefully be applied to the Andromeda. Nicias' quarrel with Pausias was not that he was a realist but that he chose small subjects; similarly Aristotle used another formula, 'our delight in mimesis', to explain works which we have connected with Pausias.

7. PORTRAITURE

These two formulae may also be applied to portraiture in art and literature. There are two elements in the first formula— 'organic composition' and 'directed at the emotions of an audience'. Of organic composition enough has already been said and it need

[1] Plutarch, *Qu. Conv.* v, 1, 2 (Overbeck, 1354).

[2] Pliny, *NH*, xxxvi, 28 (Overbeck, 1180). Winter, *KiB*, 307; Richter, *Three Critical Periods in Greek Sculpture*, fig. 48.

not be further illustrated. The artist of a portrait presents his subject so as to awake the audience's approval or disapproval, sympathy or understanding; the question here is whether in this period he solicited such reactions more urgently than his predecessors—although, of course, the earlier technique continued and no clear break can be shown. The second formula implies a new interest in external appearance, not as a term in a contrast but for itself. The contrast portraits, if our interpretation of them is right, show or imply two terms, the external appearance and something else which is essential but cannot be seen in the external appearance—the comic poet's wit or the teaching of Socrates. The new view was proclaimed in a formulation which reminds us of Plato by Lysippus, the great Sicyonian sculptor who started working in 370 or soon after. He is said to have been inspired by a chance remark of his employer Eupompus, the teacher of the painter Pamphilus, who said that the artist should imitate nature rather than another artist.[1] Lysippus himself claimed that he represented men not as they *were* but as they *appeared*. This realism was combined with an interest in composition and proportions. Lysippus, perhaps for the first time, composed three-dimensionally and for this reason too is a realist; his Apoxyomenos[2] has no single satisfactory view, and it must be appreciated as sculpture and not as relief.

Before the full bloom of early Hellenistic portraiture we have an important landmark in the Mausoleum, which was erected on the death of Mausolus in 353. Three of the figures have been identified as Mausolus, his sister Ada, and his brother Idrieus, and as a result of this recent identification we have not only the heads but also the bodies of the three official portraits.[3] The heads are

[1] Pliny, *NH*, xxxiv, 61 (Overbeck, 1444). On Lysippus' dates and career see now E. Sjöquist, *Op. Ath.* 1 (1953), 87 ff.

[2] Richter, fig. 739. Cf. Pliny, *NH*, xxxiv, 65 (Overbeck, 1508).

[3] Mausolus, Richter, fig. 228, 314 with von Lorentz, *Mausollos und die Quadriga*, 1931; Ada, British Museum, no. 1051, Winter, 303/4; Idrieus, British Museum, no. 1054, with Jongkees, *JHS*, 68 (1948), 29 ff. (I am not convinced that the traditional identification of Mausolus is wrong.)

not very different from the heads on earlier Athenian grave-reliefs of the normal type: the brows are rather more fleshy and the eyes are therefore in rather deeper shadow, the artist is more interested in the surface variations of the face. The bodies are dramatically posed: Mausolus with his sheathed sword in his left hand and his right hand outstretched, Ada with hands raised in adoration, Idrieus stepping forward with his hand raised in prayer. The three figures are fixed for posterity as they were, perhaps at a moment in a great religious ceremony. They move forwards towards the spectator and he feels their tremendous presence. This is the same quality which we noticed in Athenian painting in the middle of the century and it is clear again in Athenian grave-reliefs.[1] The figures are now in much higher relief. They are set in a gabled building which gives them a hard frame and a dark background. One figure or another faces the spectator and the grief of the parting is much more openly displayed than before. The fleshy brows with their deep shadows, the modelling of the faces, the wild hair show an obvious emotion which was scarcely seen before, and sometimes we seem to be able to detect an individual portrait.

Aristotle[2] still requires idealism in portraiture—he says that 'the good portrait painter renders the individual form but makes it more beautiful'—but even in this passage he emphasises the element of likeness. Plutarch[3] noted the distinction between idealism and realism in the portraits of Alexander. 'He gave orders that only Lysippus should make statues of him. It appears that only he communicated Alexander's character to the bronze and showed his *arete* as well as his physical appearance. The rest in the

[1] Good examples in the National Museum at Athens are (*a*) the stele of Prokleides, 737; Conze, 718; Diepolder, pl. 46; Johansen, 46, fig. 25; Buttlar, *Griechische Köpfe*, 69. (*b*) the Ilissus stele, 839; Conze, 1035; Diepolder, pl. 36; Johansen, 22, fig. 9; Buttlar, 72/3. (*c*) Axelos, 2574; Buttlar, 68.

[2] Aristotle, *Poetics*, 1454 b 9; cf. just after the end of this period Theophrastus, *Char.* ii, 12, the flatterer says that his patron's portrait is like him.

[3] *Moralia*, 335b (Overbeck, 1479). I think διάχυσις and ὑγρότης indicate 'cheerfulness, and 'mobility' rather than 'melting gaze', which seems inappropriate to Alexander.

effort to reproduce the twist of his neck and the mobility and cheerfulness of his eyes failed to preserve his masculine and leonine appearance.' Yet Lysippus claimed to be a realist: 'the older artists made men as they are, I make men as they appear.' His brother Lysistratus, according to Pliny,[1] 'was the first to take casts from living faces and then improve the wax mould made from the plaster; he was also the first to make likenesses; his predecessors had made portraits as beautiful as possible.' Apelles,[2] who painted Alexander, was said to have made portraits of 'indistinguishable likeness'. The artists themselves, their contemporaries, and later critics all felt that the portraiture of the Alexander period marked a step forward in realism beyond the idealism of older portraits, but that this realism need not be incompatible with representing the *arete* of the original. If we ask whether the critics of the time of Alexander and later had forgotten the realism of Demetrius of Alopece and the Lyme Park relief, the answer must be that this simpler realism was regarded by them as caricature. Aristotle regarded Pauson as a caricaturist and failed to appreciate that such realism was one term of a contrast.

On the evidence of the grave-reliefs the new realism depends on a more individual treatment of the head with much more surface modelling and on dramatic poses which put the figure into communication with the spectator. The treatment of the head is clearly seen in one of the few original portraits that have been preserved, the bronze boxer from Olympia.[3] On stylistic grounds this can probably be dated in the third quarter of the fourth century but the assertion that it is the Satyrus of Silanion is a mere guess. Rodenwaldt thus describes the head: 'From his features we can see and feel that he could give as good as he got. His nose and ears are punched flat; and from the knitted brows and tight-lipped mouth there speaks an unshakable will. The firm lines of

---

[1] Pliny, *NH*, xxxv, 153 (Overbeck, 1514).

[2] Pliny, *NH*, xxxv, 88 (Overbeck, 1881).

[3] Rodenwaldt, *Olympia* (in English), 1936, 49, pls. 92–3; Buschor, *Bildnisstufen*, 208; Lawrence, *Later Greek Sculpture*, 101; Picard, *IVe*, 835.

his face are framed in a wild tangle of hair and beard. His forehead and eyes bear the marks of age.' Among other portraits we may glance briefly at Alexander, the dramatic poets, and the philosophers. An original head[1] of the youthful Alexander has been attributed to Leochares; the neat hair, slightly fleshy brows, large eyes and smiling mouth do perhaps miss the masculine and leonine appearance which Plutarch requires. This we can see in the wonderful action portrait[2] of the battle between Alexander and Dareius in the mosaic copy from Pompeii; but action is not only represented in action pictures or reliefs: two bronze statuettes[3] show the wild-haired haggard Alexander in a dramatic pose with his spear.

The statesman Lycurgus, as we have said, had statues of the three great fifth-century tragedians erected in the theatre of Dionysus.[4] We know the Sophocles best. He was shown as a great Athenian gentleman in fine and carefully draped himation, but the wrinkles of the forehead and the modelling of the face show something of the controlled passion that produced the *Oedipus* and the *Antigone*. The other two wear the himation so as to have one or both shoulders bare and so set off the peculiar dignity of Sophocles. Aeschylus' head has a superb majesty, sanity, and solidity; the ecplectic quality of his plays is shown by the mask with high onkos which he carries. Euripides has thinning hair, rather close-set eyes, and high brow—a thinker and an unhappy, gloomy man. Another head of Euripides,[5] which is

---

[1] Athens, Acropolis Museum, 1331. Ashmole, *JHS*, 71 (1951), 15, pl. 11/12. A youthful head in Boston (52.1471, *Bulletin*, 51 (1953) 30) is accepted by Sjöquist as an original by Lysippus of about 330.

[2] Cf. above, p. 82 n. 3. Cf. also the Alexander sarcophagus, Richter, fig. 176.

[3] (a) Louvre. Winter, *KiB*, 334/3. (b) Grado. Von Lorentz, *RM*, 50 (1935), 333, pl. 63.

[4] Sophocles, Rome, Lateran. Richter, fig. 249; Schefold, *Bildnisse*, 90. Aeschylus, the head, Schefold, 88, with the body in the Vatican, Braccio Nuovo, 53; Pickard-Cambridge, *Festivals*, fig. 45. Euripides, the head, British Museum, 1833, Schefold, 88, with the body published by Studniczka, *JHS*, 54 (1923), 64, fig. 8.

[5] Euripides. The head, Schefold, 98; the statue is reproduced on a relief in Istanbul, Pickard-Cambridge, *Festivals*, fig. 49; *JHS*, 71 (1951), 229.

roughly contemporary, shows nothing of this tortured discontent and more of sympathetic understanding. The original was a seated statue of Euripides holding the mask of Heracles in his hand. We can, I think, understand the statue better if we consider the mask too. Sad wisdom is the mood in which Euripides might well be believed to have created his Heracles. The relation between the poet and the mask is quite different from that on the Lyme Park relief: there the disillusioned old age of the man was contrasted with the grotesque gaiety of the mask; here the sculptor still contrasts the wisdom of the poet and the unwisdom of his hero, but he is very near the action statue of the poet writing a play.

This development can be seen in the portraits of the philosophers. Lysippus made a portrait of Socrates for the Pompeion.[1] It is possible that the bust in the Terme at Rome goes back to this original. The question whether the whole statue is represented by the standing statuette in the British Museum or by the seated figure known from an old engraving seems to me insoluble. Whatever the answer may be, Poulsen is entirely right in saying: 'It is quite a different picture, quite a different man from the Platonic Socrates, not the street philosopher with the crude face, whose beauty only gradually revealed itself, but a cool, clever, presentable philosopher.' The contrast between appearance and reality which the spectator had to see in the older portrait has gone; the face itself has to show the reality through the appearance. The surviving portrait head of Aristotle[2] has now been joined to a body, and the combination may go back to the original set up by Alexander the Great. Aristotle is thinking or perhaps pausing in a lecture. Although he is seated, the left leg is partly extended and the right drawn back; the pose is not restful but energetic. He is a little man with a large head. 'From the side',

[1] Richter, *Three Critical Periods*, fig. 43; Schefold, *Bildnisse*, 82–4; Poulsen, *From the Ny Carlsberg*, 1 (1931), 33. Diogenes Laertius ii, 43 (Overbeck, 1493).

[2] Here Pl. 14. Gullini, *Arch. Class.* 1, 130 f.; Richter, *op. cit.*, fig. 44; Jaeger, *Aristotle*, 322.

says Werner Jaeger (who only knew the head), 'we are struck by the contrast between the chin jutting out beneath a tightly closed mouth, giving an expression of indomitable energy, and the critical, contemplative, perfectly level gaze of the eyes.' The energy detected in the head is revealed by the pose. If it is true that the treatises are to a considerable extent Aristotle's lecture notes, they are intelligible as the utterances of such an Aristotle. The sculptor has suggested some of the distinct elements—the certainty of rigorous pronouncement, the conscientiousness of parenthetical annotation, and the flashes of allusive illustration, which are difficult for the modern reader but must have excited the ancient audience.

Aristotle is seated lecturing, and so his statue is in direct communication with his audience like many of the other portraits of this period. The treatises are his lecture notes and occasionally we can recapture from them the essential breath of the lecture room. But the treatises were not meant for publication and therefore fall outside our survey. The question however which we have to ask is whether the later Platonic dialogues and the dialogues of Aristotle can be called portraiture in at all the same sense as the early Platonic dialogues. At first sight it seems that in the later dialogues of Plato the plot is more important than the characters. Perhaps this change should rather be phrased thus: the characters are now all friendly professionals and so only their discussion matters. The chance meetings of a mixed gathering in which Socrates then plays the leading part are abandoned for something much more like a realistic description of an Academy discussion. At the beginning of the *Theaetetus* Theaetetus is characterised as a professional, although he was too young to be a professional when Socrates met him. The frame dialogue speaks of his war service and his wounds in a battle (apparently of 369) and of his fame as a scholar; then the conversation of thirty years before between Socrates and the mathematician Theodorus begins with a description of the gifted young Theaetetus, who is neither beautiful nor rich but makes the perfect pupil. Theaetetus is thus matriculated and the discussion starts. The *Sophist* nominally carries on the next day with the addition of a professional Eleatic philosopher. The *Politicus* continues the *Sophist* with the substitution of the younger Socrates for Theaetetus, and a third dialogue was planned to complete these two. The *Timaeus* again is a meeting of friendly professionals, Socrates, Timaeus, Critias, and Hermocrates, nominally to continue the conversations of the *Republic*, and was to be completed by the *Critias* and a third dialogue. Here the form itself has changed and long speeches take the place of short give and take.

It is difficult to tell what was the form or forms of Aristotle's dialogues. It seems certain from Cicero[1] that Aristotle continued the *Timaeus* form and that he sometimes took the leading part himself. Cicero tells us that he took the leading part in the *Statesman* and *On Justice*, and this is almost certainly also true of *On Philosophy*. Thus Aristotle introduced a new realistic element. These dialogues purport to be autobiography and not historical drama like most of Plato's dialogues; the *Laws* also has a contemporary setting but Plato disguised himself as an 'Athenian stranger'. Because they are academic discussions, we can understand Basil when he says that Aristotle did not, like Plato, 'guy his characters' and Ammonius when he says that he varied the diction with the characters. His characters were professionals and the interesting part of them was their views expressed in an individual style rather than their personalities in Athenian social life. We can say very little about other characters in the dialogues: it certainly seems possible that Plato was a character in the *Nerinthus*, which is called after the Corinthian farmer who came to the Academy after reading the *Gorgias*; and in the *Eudemus*[2] which was written in 354 or very soon after, a man is addressed as 'best of all and most blessed'—he must be a king and perhaps he is a King of Cyprus, since Eudemus was a Cypriot.

In this fragment the speaker is arguing that the soul is happier

---

[1] References will be found in Rose's edition of the fragments under *I. Dialogi*.
[2] fr. 44R.

when free from the body. ' "Therefore, greatest and happiest of all men, in addition to thinking the dead blessed and happy we regard it as improper to tell lies about them or speak evil of them, as though they had already become better and greater. And this custom of ours is so old and venerable that no one knows either its beginning in time or its originator but the custom has remained continuously through endless time. In addition to this you see on men's lips that very ancient common saying." "What?" he said. And he answered, "Not to be", he said, "is the best of all things, and death is better than life. And the divinity has given us much evidence of this. For instance, they say that Midas, when after the hunt in which he captured Silenus he interrogated him and asked what is the best for men and what should be chosen in preference to everything else, at first received no answer but an unbroken silence. But when by using every means he induced him to speak, Silenus laughed aloud and said, 'Ephemeral child of a laborious daimon and cruel Fortune, why do you all compel me to speak what it is better for you not to know? For life is least painful without knowledge of one's own ills. The best of all things cannot be for men nor can they share in the nature of the best. For it is best for all men and all women not to be, and second best and first of what men can achieve is to die as soon as possible after birth.' " It is clear then that he made this declaration because existence in death is better than existence in life.'

We may contrast the smoothness and ease of this with the very concise proof that the soul is not a harmony, which is quoted from the same dialogue.[1] 'To the harmony of the body is opposed the disharmony of the body; the disharmony of the ensouled body is disease, weakness, and ugliness. Of these disease is a lack of proportion in the elements, weakness a lack of proportion in the like parts, and ugliness a lack of proportion in the organic parts. If therefore disharmony is sickness and weakness and ugliness, harmony then is health and strength and beauty. But soul is none of these things, neither health, I say, nor strength nor beauty. For

[1] fr. 45 R.

even Thersites, who was very ugly, had a soul. Then the soul is not a harmony.' It is very tempting to argue that in the two fragments we can see two different speakers characterised by their styles, but caution is imposed by the great and rather similar differences of style within the myth of Plato's *Phaedrus*.

It is not true to say that Aristotelian dialogues consisted wholly of long speeches, since we have short interjections in the *Eudemus* and in the *Nobility*.[1] Nor is it true that there was no setting since the *Eudemus* took off from an account of Eudemus' dream and death, an account which seems to have been given by Aristotle himself (*familiarem suum*),[2] and the *Grylus*[3] seems to have started with Aristotle saying that many had written praises of Grylus partly so as to please his father, Xenophon; then presumably the discussion of rhetoric got under way. These passages may have been the prologues to which Cicero refers. It is probable therefore that Aristotle's dialogues had not the extremely realistic portraiture of Plato's early dialogues but that they were dramatic in that they were presentations of a philosophical discussion and realistic in a new sense when they purported to be autobiographical. The language of the speakers was characterised, as the contemporary and rather later portraits of philosophers were characterised, and we shall not go far amiss if we think of the mosaic representing the philosophers[4] as an illustration of an Aristotelian dialogue. It does not matter to us whether they are the seven sages or seven fourth-century philosophers. They are in the open under a tree and a sundial. Five sit on a semicircular seat; two stand. One has just demonstrated something with the globe and the rest discuss it with each other. The contrast between setting and subject in the early dialogues of Plato has gone: instead we have a realistic picture of a professional discussion.

Aristotle has left us two other kinds of portraits which may be considered briefly—in the *Ethics* and in the *Constitution of Athens*.

---

[1] fr. 44, 92, 93R.   [2] fr. 37R.   [3] fr. 68R. Cf. above, p. 59.
[4] Naples, from Torre Annunziata, Schefold, 154/1 (with literature); Picard, *Mon. Piot*, 47 (1953), 87.

It is interesting to compare the successive men in Plato's *Republic*, whom we considered earlier, with the account of virtues, vices, and their possessors which Aristotle gives in the middle books of the *Ethics*. Aristotle's men, except for the *megaloprepes* and for the *megalopsychos* (who rightly reminds us of the Lateran Sophocles), are not portraits like Plato's, because he primarily wants to arrive at a definition of each virtue and vice.[1] But he gives more detail than Plato—not only professions, performance of *leitourgiai*, houses, way of living, conversation, but also voice, gestures, and dress. The method has changed; where Plato recorded a few but very characteristic details, Aristotle notes more and particularly the kind of details that are observable.[2] The magnificent man spends lavishly on dedication, buildings, and sacrifices to the gods, on equipping a chorus or a trireme, on entertaining the city, on weddings, on entertaining public guests, on his house and on beautiful and durable works of art for it. It is the picture of a very rich man, who however limits his expenditure by what is becoming, whereas the vulgar man gives a club dinner on the scale of a wedding banquet and when he equips the chorus for a comedy hangs purple curtains in the entrance to the stage. Aristotle gives some detail also of the *megalopsychos*: he is haughty with the rich and the pompous and unassuming with ordinary people. His likes and dislikes are obvious; he only deviates from the truth when he makes understatements in the popular assembly. He is not a gossip. His possessions are designed for beauty rather than profit. He would never think of hurrying away with his arms swinging; he moves slowly, his voice is deep and level. 'Vain people on the other hand are elaborate in their dress and their gestures.'

In the *Ethics* the observable details establish the value of the ethical labels. In the small-scale portraiture of the *Constitution of Athens* a detail or two make the figures come alive and ethical labels fix their value. The account of Peisistratus[3] starts with the

---

[1] Cf. D. J. Furley, *Symbolae Osloenses*, 30 (1953), 56 f.

[2] *NE*, 1122 b 20, the magnificent man; 1123 a 22, the vulgar man; 1124 b 30, the *megalopsychos*; 1125 a 30, vain men.   [3] *Ath. Pol.* 14.

keyword 'most democratic'. After describing his career (including the self-wounding, the woman dressed up as Athena, and the final seizure of power), he justifies the adjective by an account of his rule. This too is enlivened by detail, the story of the farmer whose only harvest was pain and grief and a tenth of that owed to Peisistratus, the common description of his rule as the age of Cronus, his appearance at the Areopagus and the flight of his prosecutor. Peisistratus died in his bed and his sons continued his rule. The elder, Hippias, was sensible and a ruler by nature; Hipparchus was only fond of entertainment, finding it in the arts and in love; Thessalus, who was much younger, was bold and violent. Then Aristotle tells the story of Harmodius and Aristo-geiton, ending with the change in Hippias' character so that he became harsh and ceased to trust anybody. In a brief constitu-tional history the characters only appear when they affect the constitution; a couple of adjectives sums them up and a few details make them come alive. The adjectives are ethical labels: in terms of the *Nicomachean Ethics* Hippias at the beginning of his career is the mean between the soft Hipparchus and the violent Thes-salus. The Hippias is also a brief study in development: Hippias changes from a wise ruler to a suspicious tyrant. Gossip however has no place, and Aristotle expressly denies that Solon was the lover of Peisistratus. But this denial shows that literary portraiture with a more direct approach to the emotions of the audience already existed.

Theopompus, who was about ten years younger than Aristotle, blackened his characters with as much exaggeration as his master Isocrates used in praising Evagoras and Timotheus. It is true that Dionysius of Halicarnassus[1] praises him for his discussion of justice, piety, and other virtues and for examining the passions of the soul, comparing him to a doctor who uses surgery and cautery on the diseased parts of the body, while having no concern for what is healthy. Polybius[1] however criticises him for concentrat-ing on Philip's vices after saying that he started to write on Philip

---

[1] *ad. Pomp.* 5, 7 f.   [2] Polybius, viii, 9 (ii), 1–2.

because of Philip's exceptional qualities. So in our fragments[1] we hear that Philip won the heart of the Thessalians because he was a natural buffoon, drunk every day, rejoicing in practical jokes and practical jokers; he threw away any money that he had collected; his associates were the wasters and scoundrels of the whole world; he rejected the decent characters who looked after their affairs and honoured the extravagant who spent their lives in gambling and drinking, etc., etc.; after Chaeronea he drank the whole night through and in the early morning serenaded the Athenian ambassadors. Athenian politicians and generals do not fare any better, with the exception of Peisistratus and Cimon, who belonged to an earlier and better age and threw their estates open to their fellow citizens. 'Chares was stupid and slow, and lived luxuriously too. He took flute girls, dancing-girls and *hetairai* round on his expeditions, and spent some of the war taxes on them, leaving the rest in Athens to pay the speakers, the writers of decrees, and the jurors. The Athenians did not mind this and liked him more than their fellow citizens. This was natural, because they themselves lived like this, the young wasting their time with flute girls and *hetairai*, those slightly older in drinking and dicing and similar extravagances, the whole people spending more on public feasts and meat-distributions than on good government.' It may be true that we know more of Theopompus' villains than of his heroes (and even Hermias is a villain), but it seems certain that his characters were either villains or heroes and were judged on the details of their private lives, for which he drew on such prejudiced sources as comedy.

The musical scholar, Aristoxenus of Tarentum, a man of the same generation as Theopompus, who finally became a pupil of Aristotle, also wrote his lives on the hero/villain principle.[2] Pythagoras and Archytas were heroes; Socrates and Plato were villains. We have from the *Life of Archytas* a dialogue between a

---

[1] Philip fr. 153, 217, 228 (Grenfell and Hunt); Peisistratus and Cimon fr. 89, 131; Chares fr. 235; Hermias fr. 210, 242.

[2] Archytas fr. 47 (Wehrli); Plato fr. 67, 131; Socrates fr. 51, 52, 54.

E

materialistic hedonist (in the tradition of Plato's Callicles), who had come on an embassy from the younger Dionysius, and Archytas, who answered him with a tirade against pleasure. Here we are shown the philosopher in action as in the dialogues of Aristotle and the contemporary sculptures of philosophers lecturing. Of Plato we are told that he transcribed the *Republic* from the *Antilogica* of Protagoras, and wanted to burn all the books of Democritus. Socrates started life as a stonemason; Archelaus was his lover; no one was more persuasive in voice, in face, in the character which he showed, and in his very individual appearance, but when he flamed into anger there was nothing that he would not say or do. He was passionate in love and had two wives at the same time; when they fought one another, he did not stop them but laughed at their furies with himself and with each other; at parties he was sometimes provocative, abusive, and violent. Aristoxenus quoted his source, Spintharus the tragic poet of the late fifth century, but still it is clear that he interpreted his evidence of private behaviour in the worst sense; he was accuser as much as biographer.

Solicitation of the emotions of the audience by portraiture (whether of oneself or one's client or of the other side) was part of Aristotle's theory in the *Rhetoric*.[1] Bruns[2] argued that there was a change of practice about the middle of the century and that from that time the personal element played the chief part in lawcourt speeches. The truth of this thesis can be seen by contrasting with Lysias' attack on Eratosthenes (which we have already discussed) the mutual attacks of Aeschines and Demosthenes in the speeches on the *False Embassy* made in 343 and *On the Crown* and *Against Ctesiphon* in 330. I need only recall certain points briefly. In the *False Embassy*[3] Demosthenes draws contrasting pictures of two banquets: in the first the actor Satyrus persuaded Philip to give up captives whom he had taken at Olynthus; in the second Aeschines and his drunken friends had an Olynthian woman

[1] Cf. particularly *Rhet.* 1389 a 2, 1378 a 7.   [2] *das literarische Porträt*, 552.
[3] xix, 192 ff.

horse-whipped. This is a dramatic scene like those of Lysias but it is irrelevant to the case (and probably fictitious). He goes on: 'with this on his conscience this obscene man will look you in the eyes and tell you in resounding tones of the tenor of his life. It makes me boil with indignation. Don't they know that you started by reading out the books while your mother was carrying out initiations and that in your boyhood you wallowed among orgies and drunkards? Then you were a minor clerk to the magistrates and sold your soul for two or three drachmae. Finally, instead of being a choregos yourself, you were content with the crumbs thrown to a tritagonistes.' This account of Aeschines' early life is much elaborated in the *Crown*,[1] where Aeschines starts by grinding the ink and cleaning out the schoolhouse for his father, then assists his mother in her initiations, by night dressed in a fawnskin, plastering the initiates with mud and bran, and singing ritual cries in his beautiful voice, by day leading bands of initiates through the street, waving snakes above his head, in order to get a few cakes. Then the civil service. Then he hired himself out to a couple of ranting actors and his chief reward was the fruit thrown at him by an infuriated audience.

Aeschines fights back in the same way and in particular makes much of Demosthenes' Scythian ancestry, not only in the connected account in the later speech but frequently in the earlier speech also.[2] From our point of view the detailed picture of Demosthenes' behaviour on the Embassy is perhaps the most interesting—the difficulty of having Demosthenes as a travelling companion, his boast that he would sew up Philip's mouth with an unsoaked rush, his breakdown before Philip, his attack on Aeschines after the first audience, his change of mood after the second audience when he ingratiated himself with each of his fellow ambassadors in turn. This (and much more) confirms Bruns' thesis that the personal element becomes much more important in the speeches of the second half of the fourth century and may be the decisive factor in deciding the case. For us the

[1] xviii, 258.   [2] iii, 171 f.; ii, 21 f.

comparison with the change in the technique of portraiture in stone is illuminating: we see the same shift of interest from general characteristics to observable details. Moreover the speeches explain and are explained by the later sculptured portraits of Aeschines and Demosthenes.[1] The elegant and beautifully draped Aeschines must have been very vulnerable to such descriptions (however untrue) of his youth, and the gaunt, tortured Demosthenes could have given such displays of nerves as Aeschines recounts.

The common factor in portraiture of this period is a greater interest in observable detail, for which Aristotle provided the theory when he spoke of our delight in mimesis. This may by itself be sufficient to engage the interest of the audience, but in many cases artist or writer may wish to evoke a stronger emotion, pity in the grave-reliefs, approval in the statues of great men, or hatred in rhetorical portraits of opponents; for these purposes some writers and artists are prepared to invent detail to be observed.

8. PERSONIFICATIONS

It is a curious feature of Greek art, which has led to much misinterpretation, that the Greek artist is always prepared to break his conventions and introduce something at variance with them, if he can thereby tell the spectator more than he could learn from a bare record of what was actually visible at any given moment. Even now, in spite of 'our delight in mimesis' and the achievements of the new encaustic technique in painting, the artist may introduce personifications to tell his audience more or to stir his emotions.

We have already said something of political personifications, which are both persuasive and explanatory. The City may be a person with a life of its own (like Tragedy in the *Poetics*): in the *Peace*[2] Isocrates supports his argument by saying that it is far

---

[1] Demosthenes. Richter, fig. 736. Aeschines, Schefold, 102.
[2] Isocrates, viii, 120.

more important for a city than for an individual to practise virtue and shun vice. 'A man may perhaps die before he pays the penalty for his sins; a city is immortal and undergoes chastisement both from man and from the gods.' This is both persuasive and ex-planatory, and, as earlier, no fast line can be drawn between the two uses. The element of persuasion or the desire to communicate an emotion is much stronger than the desire to explain, when Lycurgus cries in his peroration against Leocrates that the land and the trees, the harbours, the docks and the walls beg the jury for help, or Aeschines speaks of Rumour wandering unaccount-ably through Athens, or Aristotle personifies Arete as 'a maiden of beloved form' in the hymn which he wrote after the death of Hermias.[1]

When the South Italian vase-painter painted scenes from tragedy, he often included personifications of passions, which are both an explanation and a warning; sometimes we can say that they are additions by the vase-painter, sometimes they probably appeared in the tragedy itself. We have already discussed the Medea picture on an Apulian vase in Munich,[2] and as it seems to illustrate a fourth-century tragedy, we cannot tell whether Oistros standing in the chariot was an invention of the vase-painter or not. A figure,[3] who can only be Lyssa, running at Hippolytus' horses with a torch in one hand and a snake in the other while the bull rises from the sea, must surely be an addition by the painter, who remembered Euripides' description of the bull '*maddening* the team with fear'. It seems likely also that Apate (deception), who engages Tereus in conversation while the sisters speed away in chariots, is an addition by the vase-painter.[4] Apate occurs again dressed like a Fury on the *Persians* vase in Naples.[5] Here she is the folly which led Dareius to attack Greece, a folly which seduced Asia as she sits on an altar of Artemis with the result that

---

[1] *In Leocratem*, 150; Aeschines, i, 127/8; Aristotle, fr. 675 R.
[2] Cf. above p. 66 n. 1.
[3] Apulian, London, F279. Séchan, *op. cit.*, fig. 99. Euripides, *Hipp.* 1229.
[4] Apulian, Naples, 3233; *Mon. Nouv. Ann.* 1839, pl. xxi.
[5] Cf. above, p. 65 n. 2.

Artemis deserts her, but Hellas has the protection of Zeus and Athena. Hellas and Asia are personifications not so much of countries as of the people dwelling in the country; of such more examples will be quoted later. Apate and the rest, whether created by the Apulian painter or taken from the tragedy which he depicts, are parallel to the fury-passions in Plato and have tragic antecedents in the Lyssa of Euripides' *Hercules Furens* and Aeschylus' Lycurgan trilogy.

The orator Aeschines gives a modern psychological interpretation of the Furies of tragedy in the Timarchus speech:[1] 'Do not think that the impious as in tragedies are driven by Poinai, who punish them with flaming torches, but the violent pleasures of the body and the refusal to be content—these fill the pirate ships, these man the privateers, these are each man's Poine, these summon them to slaughter citizens, serve tyrants, and conspire against democracy.' On South Italian vases[2] Poinai occur both in a tragic scene (Achilles and Thersites) and in Hades standing beside Orpheus. The distinction between pictures of Hades and pictures inspired by tragedies set in Hades is probably impossible for us now to draw, but the Hades vases are certainly inspired by tragedy, whether directly or indirectly through Hades pictures. So tragedy may also have been partly responsible for pseudo-Demosthenes' description of Aristogeiton 'surrounded by the figures with which the painters surround the impious in Hades, Curse, Blasphemy, Envy, Civil Strife, and Quarrel'.[3] These are perhaps the most vivid ethical personifications in the orators, but there are many others; we may quote Demosthenes again—'in the decision of every one of you jurors love of mankind is ranged against jealousy, justice against vice, and all that is good against all that is bad.'[4]

---

[1] Aesch. i, 190. For further examples from the orators cf. R. S. Radford's Baltimore dissertation, *Personification of the use of abstract subjects in the Attic Orators and Thucydides.*

[2] Here Pl. 9. Cf. above, p. 67 n. 1, p. 43 n. 2.

[3] Demosthenes, xxv, 52.   [4] Demosthenes, xx, 165.

Such personifications are primarily persuasive; others are primarily a kind of shorthand to explain as well as sometimes to persuade. In the uncertainties of the late fifth century Tyche, which had before been Good Fortune, came more and more to mean Chance, and now Agathodaimon, Agathe Tyche and Kairos took over the old meaning or something near it. Praxiteles made statues of Agathodaimon and Agathe Tyche, and sacrifices were made to Agathe Tyche in Athens.[1] On a marble relief in Copenhagen[2] a family does reverence to Zeus Epiteleios Philios, his mother Philia, and his wife Agathe Tyche: here in the old way which goes back to Homer two fairly recent personifications (friendship and good fortune) are sanctioned by being given a divine pedigree and a very remarkable divine pedigree, justified presumably because they are felt to be so important in human affairs and have been responsible for some particular event which was the occasion for this dedication. Kairos also was the subject of a hymn by Ion of Chios in the fifth century. In the fourth century he is often personified in the orators: 'the present moment (*Kairos*) almost opens its mouth and tells you to grasp the crisis yourselves.'[3] Lysippus' statue of Kairos[4] stood on tiptoe in winged sandals, he had a razor in his right hand to recall the well-known Greek metaphor, he had a forelock to be grasped when he approached but was bald behind because once he is past no one can catch him. Thus the statue explains all the ideas which the Greeks associated with the notion of opportunity or the right moment.

The mid-fourth century is particularly the time of Eros. Plato had described and analysed Eros in the *Symposium* and characterised him as a lover; in the *Phaedrus* he gives great detail of the effect of Eros on the soul. These dialogues must have been well

---

[1] Pliny, *NH*, xxxvi, 23 (Overbeck, 1211); sacrifices, *IG*, II², 1496; cf. relief in Small Acropolis Museum, no. 391, Walter.

[2] Here Pl. 15. Copenhagen, Ny Carlsberg, Inv. 1558.

[3] Demosthenes, i, 2.

[4] Overbeck, 1463 f. gives texts, particularly *Anth. Pal.* app. 66.

known since they are clearly reflected in contemporary plays of Alexis, and other comedians discuss whether Eros is rightly painted with wings.[1] Eros in the *Symposium* behaved like a lover. Praxiteles' Eros according to an epigram[2] does not spread his magic by shooting arrows but by receiving the lovers' gaze: the interpretation is clearly right for the abstracted Praxitelean figure; in Platonic terminology he is the beauty in the beloved's soul which receives love. Scopas made a group of Pothos, Eros, and Himeros.[3] Roman copies show that his Pothos was a lover, if the marble copies have been correctly identified; his upward gaze following his raised arm expresses his longing. Only the Pothos survives, but two bronze-reliefs from hydriae[4] help us to envisage a trio—desire, preparation to awake desire, and the object of desire. Eros arranges his hair while looking into a mirror and Himeros, if we may so call him, is a winged boy dancing along and playing ball. Eros is also a lover on other bronze-reliefs;[5] sometimes he fondles a winged girl who looks away from him; sometimes he rises from a rock with a winged girl standing beside him. There are only two possible interpretations of the winged girl, Nike and Psyche. As in similar but later Hellenistic terracotta groups she has butterfly wings and is certainly Psyche, this is to be preferred. She is a personification of the soul, and this group too is inspired by Plato's description of the lover loving the beauty perceived in the soul of another.

It was suggested long ago that one of these bronze hydriae, the relief from which is illustrated here, may have held the ashes of a dead woman, whose lover has lost her until he also dies. On the relief Eros turns from the mirror in his left hand towards Psyche;

[1] Alexis 20; Aristophon 11K; Eubulus 41K.

[2] Athenaeus, 591a (Overbeck, 1255).

[3] Pausanias, i, 43, 6 (Overbeck, 1165). On copies of the Pothos see Picard, *IVe*, 653 f.

[4] New York, 44.11.9; Richter, *AJA*, 50 (1946), 363, no. 2. Berlin, 8068; Richter, *loc. cit.*, no. 1; Zuchner, *Klappspiegel*, 191 ff.

[5] Richter, *loc. cit.*, nos. 5–10. Particularly Berlin, 30071, here Pl. 13a. The interpretation as Psyche, which is rejected by Miss Richter, is accepted by Zuchner, *loc. cit.*

her arm is still on his shoulder, but she now moves away from him: the natural interpretation is that Eros has seen the dim reflection of Psyche in his mirror and therefore turns towards her but will lose her if he sees her face, as Orpheus lost Eurydice. This interpretation receives some support from the recent discovery of a contemporary bronze hydria[1] containing not only ashes but an 'Orphic' tablet instructing the dead how to proceed in the Underworld. The relief on the new hydria (as on several others) showed the wind god Boreas carrying off the Attic maiden Oreithyia, and this story was evidently used as an allegory for the flight of the soul into the air at death.

These overtones we can only appreciate through this chance of a lucky discovery. In daily life love may occur at a symposium or at a Dionysiac festival. We have a longhand and a shorthand version of each. A vase in Naples[2] represents a symposium with all the skill in showing varied moods that the artist could muster. On the first couch one young man is trying to win a *hetaira* from another; on the second love is just beginning; on the third a youth and *hetaira* are kissing; the host looks on. But to make the situation clear the painter has added four Erotes. In a picture in the Tholos of Epidaurus[3] Pausias painted Eros with a lyre, his bow and arrows laid aside, and beside him Methe (Intoxication) drinking from a glass cup: this is shorthand for the symposium of youths and *hetairai*, such as we have just seen on the Attic vase. Love, as we know from New Comedy, may occur in a Dionysiac procession or at a Dionysiac festival. We have two versions by a single painter:[4] in one the women are preparing their offerings, a satyr shows that they are preparing for a Dionysiac procession, and Eros shows that love is involved. The other (like Pausias' picture of Eros and Methe) is in shorthand: on the left Eros tying his sandal as anyone must who takes part in a procession, then the

---

[1] *Arch. Eph.* 1950/1, 80. For the relief cf. Richter, *loc. cit.*, nos. 17–21.

[2] Naples, 2202, Metzger, 363/41; Schefold, *U.*, no. 108.

[3] Pausanias ii, 27, 3 (Overbeck, 1761). Contrast Picard, *IVe*, 258. Cf. above, p. 83.

[4] Both in New York, 06.1021.181. Metzger, 350/5; Schefold, *U.*, no. 593. 25.190. Here Pl. 16. Metzger, 349/4; Schefold, *U.*, no. 327.

processional basket, then Pompe (Procession), a beautiful naked woman holding a laurel branch, and Dionysus seated looking at her. Thus beside the realistic representation of emotion in the faces and attitudes of the actors there exists the other method of personifying the emotion and characterising the personification by giving it the emotion which it personifies. So far from being excluded by the new realism, personification lives on as a further means of explaining the artist's or writer's intention and persuading his audience to accept it.

At the end of our period, in 327 B.C. or soon after, the painter Aetion painted the marriage of Alexander and Rhoxane:[1] in this picture one smiling Eros pulled aside Rhoxane's veil, another untied her sandal, another tugged at Alexander's cloak; other Erotes played with Alexander's arms, two carrying his spear, two more carrying a third on his shield, and another lying in ambush beneath his overturned breastplate. Here the Erotes are no longer simply symbols of love but have taken on a new life of their own which looks forward ultimately to the *putti* of the Renaissance.

9. CONCLUSION

The Erotes playing with Alexander's arms clearly belong to the Hellenistic age and visibly show us how far we have come from the classical world of young Plato, old Aristophanes, and the sculptor Cephisodotus. Athens has ceased to be an imperial state and is now at best a free ally of a Macedonian king. Idealist philosophy has yielded much of her territory to logic, science, psychology, and scholarship. Tragedy is on the way to becoming a hieratic survival. Comedy is nearly ready to perform part of tragedy's earlier task with the comedy of manners. Art has restated in a new classical style the 'dignity of heroes', while at the same time perfecting the means of portraying physical appearance and psychological phenomena.

The more I have learned about this period the more I have

[1] Lucian, *Herod.* 4 (Overbeck, 1938).

become convinced of the overwhelming greatness of Aristotle. As the pupil of Plato and the tutor of Alexander, he is the centre of the revolution in Greek thought which converted the Classical into the Hellenistic age. Some of the results in literature and art will be discussed in the next chapter. In this chapter we have found that, whether we are considering tragedy or comedy, painting or sculpture, or prose style, we can never get very far from him. Scholarship would not have existed if he had not transferred the technique of biology to the problems of literature (and, to a smaller degree, of art). But the biological outlook also made it possible for him not only to divert Platonic philosophy in a new direction and into the new channels of logic and science but to accept as existent and therefore considerable much that Plato had rejected in art, literature, and political institutions. Tragedy flourished and must therefore be explained. The individual tragedy or sculpture could be seen as a universal particularised in the same sort of way as the individual member of a biological species. Purposeful organic composition was a term equally applicable to nature as a whole, an individual animal, tragedy as a historical growth, or the individual play or speech. Thus the young bio-logist and philosopher could take the chair of rhetoric at the Academy and at the same time write the first drafts of the *Poetics*. It was helpful, of course, that recent practice in art and literature was readily amenable to his theories and that, as I believe, a first-rate practitioner and theorist came to the Academy in the person of the older Theodectes. But part of Aristotle's greatness was the ability to accept and appreciate data of whatever kind and to adopt and adapt the work of others.

In 323 Alexander died and for a moment democratic indepen-dence flared up in Athens. Aristotle yielded before the storm, bequeathing to the new Athens Theophrastus and Menander.

IV

Art and Literature in Theophrastus' Athens

1. DEMETRIUS OF PHALERUM

IF the tradition that Theophrastus heard Plato is true, he must have come to Athens before he was twenty-three years old, and must have been in Athens while Plato was writing the *Laws*. It has been suggested that he started a collection of Greek laws as soon as he came to Athens;[1] such a collection may well have been useful to Plato, was used by Aristotle in the *Politics* and the *Constitution of Athens*, and was later the basis of Theophrastus' own great work on *Laws* and of the policy of his pupil Demetrius of Phalerum. He probably followed Aristotle on his wanderings, and was certainly with him at the Lyceum. He took over the school when Aristotle withdrew to Chalcis in 322, and ensured the continuity of Aristotelian teaching and research until his death thirty-five years later. To this central core of thought and its relation to contemporary art and literature we shall return later.

Our period then may be taken as the thirty-five years that Theophrastus was head of the Peripatetic school, a period longer by some five years than the working life of his pupil Menander. It starts with Athenian defeat on land and sea and the imposition by Antipater of an oligarchic constitution with a greatly restricted franchise. Then in 319 Antipater died and the Athenians again hoped for freedom; the leading oligarchs, including Demetrius of Phalerum, fled and were condemned to death in their absence, and Theophrastus was put on trial for impiety and acquitted. But in 317 the Athenians had to come to terms with Antipater's son

---

[1] Bloch, *Harvard Studies*, suppl. vol. i, 357.

Cassander, and Demetrius of Phalerum was made governor of Athens. He again restricted the franchise, though not so violently as Antipater, and governed on approved Peripatetic principles, interfering with the number of guests that people asked to dinner and the amount of money that they spent on public festivals and private funerals. Three hundred and sixty statues were erected to him, we are told, in three hundred days (but this may be gossip), and in the procession at the Great Dionysia in his archonship a poem was sung in which he was called 'excessively noble and sun-like';[1] but however much flattery some people were prepared to accord him, the comic poets, even the pro-Macedonian Timocles and the gentle Menander, his fellow-pupil under Theophrastus, made fun of his *gynaikonomoi* and their invasion of individual privacy.[2]

In 307 Demetrius of Phalerum was expelled amid wild rejoicing. Demetrius the tyrant is an unattractive figure. Demetrius the philosopher has some interest. He was an 'arts' man and the fragments of his writings show no trace of the scientific bent which is so clear in Aristotle and Theophrastus. Most of his written work, as far as we can apprehend it, shows some relation to his career as a politician trained in the Peripatetic school. Whereas his list of Athenian archons was a purely historical work of the same kind as the Aristotelian records of victors, his *Athenian lawgiving* seems to have shown the place of his own laws at the end of a historical development,[3] and his defence of his own *Ten years' rule* was in rhetorical style: 'the tripod', he said in defending his laws about the choregia, 'was not a dedication of victory but a last libation from exhausted riches and a cenotaph of bankrupt fortunes.'[4] As an orator, Cicero saw him as skilful in argument, not sufficiently forceful, but pleasant and recognisably a pupil of Theophrastus.[5] Understandably, therefore, in his *Rhetoric*[6] he criticised the vul-

---

[1] Athenaeus, 542e, quoting Duris of Samos.
[2] Cf. *Studies in Later Greek Comedy*, 103.
[3] Cf. Bayer, *Demetrios Phalereus*, 159.　　　　[4] fr. 136 Wehrli.
[5] fr. 73 cf. 175 ff.　　　　[6] fr. 162, 166, 175.

garity of Demosthenes' delivery (he is our authority for the story of the pebbles), but at the same time recognised the necessity of adapting style to suit different kinds of audience.

Certainly before 290, and therefore probably during the first ten years of his exile, he wrote about *Tyche*: 'Would either the Persians or the Macedonians have believed fifty years ago, if some god had foretold them the future, that today the Persians, who then ruled the world, would have scarcely a name, while the Macedonians, who were never named then, would now be masters of the world?'[1] Here too, as in his political treatises, he evidently saw his own vicissitudes as part of a historical development. The quotation ends: 'Tyche, who makes no covenants with us mortals but surprises us by innovations contrary to our calculations and shows her power in the unexpected, now seems to me to show all men, by putting the Macedonians to live among Persian riches, that they too have only been lent these benefits, until she has a new plan for them.' This is summed up by another fragment[2] in which Tyche leading Wealth is described as the blind leading the blind. Tyche, as a personification of Chance, is peculiarly relevant to Demetrius' own life but also to the many changes of fortune in the Hellenistic age. We have seen something of her past history. In the adventures of New Comedy she naturally plays a considerable role, and, as the prologue figure of Menander's *Heauton Penthon*,[3] announces that she is 'competent to determine and dispose all these things'. Theophrastus himself was criticised by Cicero[4] for giving too much importance to fortune in his account of the happy life. Here then we have not only the survival and revival of an old personification but also a sign of a shift of interest from the typical to the individual, because Tyche is the unique combination of circumstances which at a particular time and place is the decisive environment for a particular person.

The death of Cassander, his former patron, in 298–7 presumably extinguished Demetrius' hopes of governing Athens again and he accepted an invitation from Ptolemy Soter to come to

[1] fr. 81.   [2] fr. 80.   [3] Cf. *Studies in Menander*, 199.   [4] *De Fin.* v, 5.

Alexandria. Here he could play the part of philosopher attached to king, a relationship not uncommon in the Hellenistic world, which was the practical realisation of Plato's ideal philosopher king. He did not, like Aristotle, look after the king's son; for that he persuaded Ptolemy to invite Straton, who later succeeded Theophrastus as head of the Peripatetic school. His most important achievement in Alexandria was the foundation of the library. Although the direct references to this are late and overlaid with unlikely details, Strabo[1] says that Aristotle was the earliest known book collector and taught the kings in Egypt how to arrange a library. Strabo evidently saw the library at Alexandria as the direct descendant of Aristotle's library, and Demetrius of Phalerum is the obvious connecting link between the beginning of scholarship in Athens and its great flowering in Alexandria. To this time perhaps belong his works on Homer, in which he gave some curious information about pre-Homeric singers and criticised Homer's character drawing.[2]

2. ALEXANDRIA AND TRAGEDY

Alexandria does not concern us except in so far as we need it to complete our picture of Athens in the early Hellenistic age. In Demetrius of Phalerum we see one link between the two cities. Theophrastus himself refused Ptolemy's invitation just as Menander refused. But another great comic poet, Philemon, went to Egypt, and the fragments of his *Panegyris*[3] both recall Theocritus: in one somebody asks 'did the king make the highway for you alone?' and in the other somebody complains that an Egyptian has soiled his or her cloak. At this time, early in the reign of Ptolemy Philadelphus, Egypt had its own guild of Artists of Dionysus,[4] including tragic and comic poets and actors, a dancer, a technical

[1] Strabo, XIII. i., 54, 608c.   [2] fr. 190–3.

[3] frs. 58–9K. Cf. also the Strobilos fragments, *Studies in Later Greek Comedy*, 142 f.

[4] Cf. Pickard-Cambridge, *Festivals*, 289 f. For Athens itself the evidence of Demosthenes, xix, 192 and Aristotle, *Rhet.* 1405 a 23 cannot be disregarded, cf. also above, p. 30.

man, a clerk, and patrons. The institution was probably already some eighty years old in Athens, and therefore the organisation as well as the drama was imported. The development of these guilds all over the Greek world in the third century is evidence of the high regard in which drama was held.

Tragic poets and tragic actors were great figures, whose portraits were painted by the best artists.[1] The picture of a tragic actor clothed as a young king, with purple cloak, sword, and sceptre, with his mask beside him, undoubtedly goes back to an original of this time, because his face is like the portraits of Alexander's successors and the girl looks like a Tanagra figure. Another picture shows a tragic poet contemplating the mask of a young hero (it is perhaps the Philicus of Protogenes), and on a late Hellenistic silver cup Lycophron considers the mask and the prophetic cauldron of Cassandra. But although poets undoubtedly gave themselves airs, it is unlikely that new tragedy amounted to very much in the Hellenistic age.

The Cynic tragedies,[2] in which Diogenes justified incest and cannibalism, and Crates 'expressed the noble stamp of his philosophy', belonged to a different genre altogether, and have nothing to do with the theatre. The Pleiad belong mainly to the third century and to Alexandria but some of them seem also to have produced in Athens. Of them Philicus was a considerable lyric poet;[3] he was painted as a tragic poet by Protogenes and led the Artists of Dionysus in the great festival at the beginning of the reign of Ptolemy Philadelphus. It is possible that he wrote the *Themistocles* which is ascribed by Suidas to the comic poet of the same name. Sositheus wrote a *Daphnis or Lityerses*, which must

---

[1] The actor Gorgosthenes was painted by Apelles; cf. Pickard-Cambridge, *Festivals*, fig. 43. The tragic poet, Philicus, was painted by Protogenes, cf. *op. cit.*, fig. 44. Lycophron and Cassandra, cf. below, p. 113 n. 3. Cf. *Greek Theatre Production*, nos. A57, 58, 55.

[2] Cf. Dudley, *History of Cynicism*, 25 f.; R. Höistad, *Cynic Hero and Cynic King*, 143.

[3] Cf. J. U. Powell, *New Chapters*, iii, 195 ff.; K. Latte, *Mus. Helv.* 11 (1954), 1 f.

have been a satyr-play to judge from the tone of the two fragments, but is remarkable for the extreme strictness of its versification—there is no resolution of long syllables in the twenty-
four preserved lines. Sositheus, also presumably in a satyr-play,
spoke of the Stoics as 'oxen driven by Cleanthes' folly', for which,
according to Diogenes Laertius,[1] he was howled down. Contemporary allusion is unexpected in a satyr-play, but already in 424
the author of the *Agen*, which was produced for Alexander on the
Hydaspes, described the temple built by Harpalus for the *hetaira*,
Pythionice. For the Pleiad itself we can also quote the *Menedemus*
of Lycophron, in which Silenus described to his children the
satyrs the unsatisfactory banquets held by Menedemus. In these
fragments of the *Menedemus* there is no lack of resolved syllables,
but in four lines quoted from Lycophron's *Pelopidae* and in his
monologue *Alexandra* the metre is as strictly observed as by
Sositheus; there are only about twenty resolved syllables in nearly
fifteen hundred lines of the *Alexandra*.[2] The *Alexandra* is unique,
a monologue in cruelly stilted and allusive language, in which a
slave reports Cassandra's prophecies to Priam: the prophecies
reach down to Lycophron's own time. Recent scholarship seems
to have shown that there is nothing incompatible with a date early
in the third century, and on a Hellenistic silver cup (as we have
noted) Lycophron contemplates the tragic mask and the cauldron
of Cassandra.[3] Three points may be noticed—the stiffness of the
metre, the monologue form (we may ask whether some such non-
dramatic form had already been used in Theodectes' *Mausolus*),
and the contemporary allusions (however difficult they may be to
interpret). Lycophron also wrote a *Cassandrians*: the name must
refer to the foundation of Cassandria in 316, again contemporary
or very recent history.

[1] Diog. Laert. 7, 173.

[2] Koster, *Traité de métrique grecque²*, 112; Wilamowitz, *Hellenistische Dichtung*, ii, 148.

[3] Cf. particularly A. Momigliano, *JRS*, 32 (1942), 57; *CQ*, 39 (1945), 49;
Ch. Picard, *Actes du Ier Congrès de la F.I.A.E.C.*, 191, and *Mon. Piot*, 44
(1950), 53.

Another poet, Moschion,[1] shows two of these characteristics, extreme strictness of metre and choice of historical subjects. He not only wrote a *Pheraeans* (presumably the subjects of the tyrant Jason who died in 370), but also a *Themistocles*. We have already noted that Philicus may have written a *Themistocles*, and Diphilus wrote a comedy called *Amastris*, in which Themistocles' daughter was called 'Athenian guest'.[2] It is in this context that the puzzling fragment of a Gyges drama[3] recently published belongs. The arguments need not be repeated here. It may suffice to notice that, if we want a parallel in tragedy for its metrical peculiarities, the nearest parallels are in the fragments of Sositheus, Lycophron, and Moschion, and the *Alexandra* of Lycophron. The language is archaic in flavour; the treatment of the subject is closely modelled on Herodotus' account of Gyges and Candaules' wife. In the fragment Candaules' wife tells how she had seen Gyges in the royal bedchamber at night and has summoned him after sending the king about his morning business. How the play went on we cannot say; it may well be that, as Lesky suggests, a parallel in technique is afforded by Ezekiel's tragedy on the Exodus; in that case unity of time may have been disregarded and much of Herodotus' story included, giving far more events and less action than we are accustomed to in Greek tragedy. A slight analogy is afforded by the length of prophecy in the *Alexandra* of Lycophron. This however is speculation; but it is certain that Hellenistic tragedy showed extreme strictness of versification, some experiments in form, and some flights into comparatively recent history for subjects.

When we have said this, we have said most of what can be said. It has been reckoned that we know the names of sixty poets who wrote tragedy during the last three centuries B.C.[4] Of these sixty

---

[1] On the dating see *RE* s.v. Moschion; Wilamowitz, *op. cit.*, 149 n. 1.

[2] Diphilus fr. 10K. Cf. *Studies in Later Greek Comedy*, 153.

[3] Lobel, *PBA*, xxxv, 1; Page, *New Chapter in the History of Greek Tragedy*; Latte, *Eranos*, 48 (1950), 131; Lesky, *Hermes*, 81 (1953), 1.

[4] Cf. Weinreich, *Epigrammstudien*, i, 1948, 44; Ziegler, *RE*, vi, 2, 1971. On Hellenistic tragedy in general see now P. Venini, *Dioniso*, 16 (1953), 3 ff.

only nineteen are known from literature and only three are mentioned in Hellenistic epigrams on poets. Their production was no doubt considerable, but it is difficult to believe that it would have vanished so completely if it had had merit. We have some evidence that early in the third century classical tragedies were given more place than before at the Athenian Dionysia. Sometime between 287 and 275[1] the formula used in inscriptions which record the crowning of benefactors at the Dionysia changed from 'at the tragic competition' to 'at the new tragic competition'; the new tragic competition means the competition of new tragedies. It implies that there had been introduced by this time a competition of old tragedies instead of the single old tragedy which was given at each festival from 386. Moreover, for three years about 250 B.C.,[2] we have again a record on stone of dramatic contests in Athens and in these years three old satyr-plays and three old tragedies were produced instead of one each in the years 341–339. This surely suggests that classical tragedy had become more important in relation to new tragedy than it had ever been before. Moreover the comic poets give us some idea of the veneration in which classical tragedy was held from 320 onwards: 'fifth-century tragedy, partly because of Lycurgus and Aristotle, had become a classic well known to the poet (Menander) and his audience. It was a classic which Menander's characters could quote as a repository of wisdom or as a means of making their words more impressive, a classic, moreover, to which Menander could allude and be sure that his audience, perceiving the allusions, would understand the likeness and the unlikeness of a particular comic to a particular tragic situation.'[3] Aristotle's rules did in fact help to form a great new drama, whose potency is still alive, but that was not New Tragedy but New Comedy. I think we can probably say that the

[1] *IG*, II, i, 657, seems to be the last dated example of the old formula; 682, the first of the new. The references to 'new tragedies' in 336 are illusory: Demosthenes, xviii, 54 is not a genuine document and the 'new' in some manuscripts of Aesch. iii, 34, is not supported by the parallel passages in 41 and 154.

[2] Merritt, *Hesperia*, 7 (1938), 116 f.; Körte, *Hermes*, 73 (1938), 123; Pickard-Cambridge, *Festivals*, 123.   [3] *Studies in Menander*, 194.

result of Lycurgus' policy and Aristotle's theory was to kill the creative force of new tragedy, conserve classical tragedy as a hieratic survival, and assist the birth of New Comedy.

3. THE PHILOSOPHERS

In 307, as we have said, Demetrius of Phalerum was expelled amid wild rejoicing. Theophrastus had to retire because of a law, directed chiefly at the Peripatetics and the Academics, that no one should preside over a philosophical school without the permission of the Boule and Demos; in the next year the law was found to be inconsistent with Solon's principle of freedom of association and the philosophers returned. 'Menander was very nearly condemned because he was the friend of Demetrius of Phaleron',[1] but a cousin of Demetrius Poliorcetes begged him off. Demetrius Poliorcetes, who was the son of Antigonus Monophthalmus and the father of Antigonus Gonatas, and dominated Athenian politics at various times and for various periods between 307 and his death in 285, was a brilliant soldier and a gay spirit. He claimed to be descended from Poseidon, and the bronze which has been identified as his statue by Lysippus' pupil, Tisicrates, is a young version of a well-known Poseidon often attributed to Lysippus.[2] When he arrived in Athens in 290, he was greeted by a processional chorus of the same kind as had flattered Demetrius of Phalerum in his archonship.[3] They described him as 'gay and beautiful and smiling, as is right for a god'; 'Hail, son of the most mighty god Poseidon and of Aphrodite. Other gods are either far away or have no ears or do not exist or do not attend to us at all. But thee we see in our midst, not wood nor stone but flesh and blood.' This is flattery but not therefore entirely unrevealing. In the vicissitudes of the wars between Alexander's successors the traditional

[1] Diogenes Laertius, 5, 79.

[2] Naples, 1211 (5026). Picard, *RA*, 22 (1944), 6. Tisicrates, Pliny, *NH*, xxxiv, 67 (Overbeck, 1525). The Poseidon: Rome, Lateran, Richter, *Three Critical Periods*, fig. 29.

[3] Athenaeus, 253c–d, partly from Duris of Samos, cf. V. Ehrenberg, *Aspects of the Ancient World*, 179 f.

gods seemed peculiarly unhelpful; they were wood and stone. Or they did not exist, as some philosophers said. Or they paid no attention to men, as Epicurus said now and Aristotle had implied. The Hellenistic ruler, however, was a real power for good or ill, and here we can detect such genuine feeling as lies behind the deification of Hellenistic rulers and behind the excessive flattery of allowing Demetrius Poliorcetes to live with his mistresses in the Parthenon and erecting altars to them and his favourites. The philosophers had destroyed the old beliefs without substituting anything for the ordinary educated person. This is not however entirely true of Epicureanism or Stoicism, the two new philosophies which were both established in Athens in the five years after the expulsion of Demetrius of Phalerum.

It is the common opinion that they were rather 'ways of life' than philosophies in the Aristotelian sense. The new feature, which is common both to them and to the Cynics, is the direct appeal to the ordinary man to live in a certain way. To this direct ethical command all else was subordinated, however much knowledge this or that thinker demanded or displayed to sanction it. They were thus (and some of them consciously) heirs of Socrates the street philosopher. They are concerned with the private individual in his ordinary life and with politics, physics, or metaphysics only as they affected the private life of the ordinary man. Theophrastus defined comedy as dealing with 'the events of everyday life' and the definition can well be applied to the Hellenistic philosophers. Epicurus adopted the atomism of Democritus as his physical theory, because he could thereby banish the two great fears of men, fear of death and fear of divine action. So 'the blessed and immortal nature (i.e. the gods) knows no trouble itself nor causes trouble to another, so that it is never constrained by anger or favour'.[1] 'Death is nothing to us; for that which is dissolved is without sensation and that which is without sensation is nothing to us.'[2] He had no interest in science for itself but only as a means to peace of mind. The atoms of the physical world move beyond

---

[1] Epicurus, *KD*, 1.   [2] *KD*, 2.

our control, and therefore we need not fear because we cannot influence them. We can however control our own mental world, and secure freedom from disturbance both by retiring from active life and by choosing those pleasures which consist of absence of pain in the body and absence of confusion in the soul.[1] The comic poets mocked at Epicurus for pursuing bodily pleasure, but he himself said:[2] 'The pleasant life is not produced by a chain of drinking-parties and revels, nor by sexual indulgence, nor by fish and all the other elements in a rich menu, but by sober calculation which searches out the reasons for every choice and expels the false opinions which most confound the soul.' The gentleness of this wisdom, which prefers to retire rather than to condemn, Epicurus shares with Theophrastus and Menander and some of the best artists of the time. The contemporary portrait[3] shows something of the struggles by which 'sober calculation' is accompanied and something of the calm achieved.

Zeno is a less attractive figure, 'sour, bitter, frowning, and mean',[4] the sort of preacher whom the fashionable go to hear and who receives honours from popular assemblies and kings. When he first came to Athens, we are told, he was reading Xenophon's *Memorabilia* in a bookshop one day and asked the bookseller where such men as Socrates were to be found; the bookseller pointed out the Cynic Crates, and Zeno became his pupil. He did not, however, like the Cynic's lack of social decorum. To cure him Crates told him to carry a pot of soup through the Ceramicus; when Zeno tried to conceal it under his cloak, Crates broke it with his stick, and as Zeno ran away with soup streaming down his legs, Crates cried out, 'Why are you running away, little Phoenician? Nothing so very bad has happened to you.' Crates[5] was a rich man who had given up his fortune to become a Cynic

---

[1] *KD*, 14; *Ep.* 3, 131.   [2] *Ep.* 3, 132.

[3] New York, 11.90 etc. Schefold, *Bildnisse*, 118, 121/1.

[4] Diogenes Laertius, vii, 16. His bust is in Naples in two versions: Schefold, *Bildnisse*, 108, 209.

[5] Cf. Dudley, *Cynicism*, 42 f. and Diogenes Laertius for texts. The picture: Rome, Terme, Schefold, *Bildnisse*, 162, 215.

philosopher; he had a complete scorn of pretensions, intellectual and otherwise; and lived in Athens a life of practical and helpful asceticism, which his wife, Hipparchia, contrary to all conventions, shared with him. We have a charming picture, which perhaps goes back to a contemporary original, of Crates setting out with his wallet and his bedding and Hipparchia following with her little basket on her head.

Zeno, however, left Crates in 301–0 to set up his own school in the Stoa Poikile. He went back two hundred years to Heraclitus for his physical theories, adding the doctrine of a periodical world conflagration and deriving from them an ethical theory with one great command: 'live according to nature.' Nature for him is God =Fire=the Soul of the Universe, of which our soul is a fragment. The power of this god, immanent in the Universe, is complete and therefore our free will only consists in our willingness to act in accordance with it; we shall act in accordance with it whether we like it or not. Moreover, there is an absolute distinction between good and bad and no gradations between them; the wise man who has decided to live in accordance with nature is given all the offices associated with earthly success. He is king and general and statesman and everything else. This rigid and uncompromising doctrine did not prevent Cleanthes, Zeno's successor, from clothing the Stoic god in the trappings of the traditional Zeus, and when he was faced with the heliocentric system of Aristarchus of Samos, he said its author should be indicted for impiety.[1]

In the Lyceum under Theophrastus, however, pure research continued over a very wide field. His own energy and productivity were immense, and in botany, rhetoric, and legal science at least he provided a new foundation for future thought. Modern scholarship has reclaimed much for him personally from the general corpus of Peripatetic writing by careful comparison with works definitely attested as his, expecially with the *Causes of Plants*, and

[1] The chief fragments of Zeno on which the above account is based are Von Arnim, i, 179, 157, 102, 216, 224.

has shown him to be a thinker of first-rate importance and not merely a pale shadow of Aristotle. As they worked together for thirty years it is difficult, if not impossible, to disentangle entirely Theophrastus' contribution. He certainly preserved a great deal, but he also developed it along lines which were beginning to appear in the later stages of his master's work. Here we can only pick out a few leading ideas and try to see them in relation to contemporary art and literature. It would not, I think, be wrong to start with the passage in Aristotle's *Ethics*[1] where he says 'Nature seems to have made friendliness inhere in the parent towards its offspring and in the offspring toward its parent (not only among men but also among birds and most animals) and in fellow racials towards each other, and in men towards men, for which reason we praise the philanthropic. One can see on one's travels how friendly and close to his fellow every man is.' The word translated 'close' is *oikeion*, which is central for Theophrastus. He extends the 'closeness' to link up the whole living world of plants, animals, and men,[2] which somehow fits together into a purposive scheme for survival and preservation of the species.[3] Happiness consists in the 'unhindered exercise of perfect *arete* on objects which conform to one's nature', i.e. on things which are 'close' to one, and one 'perfects one's own nature when one gains by *techne* what one does not possess, such as food of the right kind and amount and the removal of hindrances and obstacles'.[4] Everything has by nature an instinct (*horme*) for the good, as can be seen from children, who have not yet attained reason,[5] and a 'closeness' to some parts of its environment, as some trees show affection for each other: the olive and the myrtle have intertwined roots and the shoots of the myrtle come up through the boughs of the olive.[6]

[1] *NE*, 1155 a 16.

[2] Ap. Porph. *de Abstinentia*, 3, 25. Cf. Bernays, *Theophrastos Schrift über die Frommigkeit*, 96, 101; Walzer, *N. Phil. Unters.* 7 (1929), 259.   [3] *CP*, II, xvii, 9.

[4] Stobaeus, ii, 130, 20; *CP*, I, xvi, 11 (Dirlmeier, 'Oikeiosislehre', *Philologus*, Supplt. xxx, 68).

[5] Aristotle, *MM*, 1206 b 17 and *CP*., *loc. cit.*, cf. Dirlmeier, *op. cit.*, 45.

[6] *CP*, III, x, 4.

The factor of environment is very important: 'sex, soil, climate, and nutriment in general cause differences in plants, for which reason specialised kinds come into being and often what is contrary to nature becomes normal when it has endured and increased in quantity.'[1]

Three ideas in these passages are of very general application: first the idea of 'closeness', which implies the linking together of all individual living things and in the philosopher an affectionate regard for their individuality, secondly the idea of growth to perfection along lines dictated by natural instinct but both influenced by environment and assisted by *techne*, and thirdly the emphasis on the gradualness of growth and the smallness of the interval between different kinds of living things and therefore an insistence on minor subdivisions rather than broad general categories.[2]

We have already noticed that Aristotle transferred the biological idea of organic growth to the history of art and literature, and sketched the beginnings of a literary and artistic history on these lines in the *Poetics*.[3] Theophrastus himself seems to have proceeded at least to some extent historically in his book on *Style*, since we know that he noted Herodotus and Thucydides as an important stage in the development of historical writing and credited Thrasymachus with the invention of certain kinds of rhythm and a certain kind of style.[4] It is unfortunate that we only know his works on rhetoric and his very important work on *Style* from brief and scattered fragments. But he evidently distinguished more stages in the development of historical writing than Aristotle, who mentions Herodotus only as an example of the 'strung-together' style. Theophrastus saw in Herodotus and Thucydides the beginning of 'a more copious and ornate' historical style. Under the heading of ornament he included at least

---

[1] *CP*, IV, xi, 7.
[2] Cf. Regenbogen, *RE*, s.v. Theophrastos, 1470; Dirlmeier, *op. cit.*, 66.
[3] Cf. above, p. 54.
[4] Cic. *Or.* 39, 172 (cf. Dion. Hal. *Dem.* 3; *Lysias*, 6). Cf. Regenbogen, *op. cit.*, 1530. New papyrus fragments: Hibeh 183, Hamburg 128.

'the fitting together of words' and 'the figures which comprehend them'.[1] Words are to be fitted together so as to avoid hiatus and to give certain pleasing rhythms. The 'figures' include particularly antithesis and the like. On these Theophrastus gave two judgments[2] which have been preserved: he said that the pursuit of exact balance in clauses was unsuitable to a serious subject-matter and robbed the style of its effect; his example is taken from a speech of Lysias which is probably spurious, but we may ask whether Plato's treatment of Lysias in the *Phaedrus* lies behind this choice. Secondly, he admired 'the compactness of thought and neatness of expression which was suitable for the law-courts and every real contest'. Of this he found the first example in the fifth-century sophist Thrasymachus. Dionysius thought that Lysias was its inventor; priority does not concern us, but if Dionysius was interpreting Theophrastus correctly, we can claim that Theophrastus prized the brevity and economy which we regard as characteristic of the best Greek prose. Theophrastus would seem to have been more concerned with the elements of good style than with historical development and distinguished nicely between words that were beautiful and words which were not.[3] But we have noticed that he gave Herodotus, Thucydides, and Thrasymachus their place as innovators, and this implies also that he distinguished between historical and rhetorical prose. In fact we may see here an instance of the further subdivision of classes which is remarkable in Theophrastus' botany. Yet more important is his clear distinction between poets and orators on the one hand and philosophers on the other: poets and orators were concerned with the relation of words to hearers, whereas philosophers were concerned with the relation of words to subject-matter.[4] This would certainly not be true of the Cynics nor of many fragments of the Stoics, but Theophrastus had no reason to concern himself with them. It is however the charter of the plain

[1] Dion. Hal. *de Isocr.* 3.   [2] Dion. Hal. *de Lysia*, 14; 6.
[3] Dion. Hal. *de Comp.* 16; Demetrius, *On Style*, 173; and a new Hibeh fragment, no. 183.   [4] fr. 64/5 W.

scientific style, which had a long history behind it when Theophrastus used it in his botany.

In the Hellenistic period 'the idea of growth to perfection along lines dictated by natural instinct but both influenced by environment and assisted by *techne*' was evidently applied to histories of art. The biological scheme is particularly clear in those parts of the accounts of painting and sculpture in Pliny's *Natural History*[1] which have been traced back to Xenocrates, a sculptor pupil of Lysippus but probably an Athenian by birth and a contemporary of Theophrastus; there we find for instance that 'Pheidias first opened the way to the art of bronze casting and Polycleitus perfected it';[2] this is an account of a critical moment in the history of fifth-century sculpture. In the history of painting we may note first an early moment, perhaps the beginning of the seventh century: 'the drawing of outlines, which was invented by Cleanthes of Corinth, was developed by Aridices of Corinth and Telephanes of Sicyon, who used sparing inner markings and added inscriptions.' Secondly, in the later sixth century 'Eumarus of Athens was the first to distinguish men from women and Cimon of Cleonae exploited his discoveries and invented three-quarter faces'. Later, in the fifth century 'Polygnotus was the first to paint women in transparent clothes and vary the archaic stiffness of expression . . . Parrhasius first gave symmetry to painting'.[3] The scheme is the same as we have seen in Theophrastus' botany—a first start made by a genius (*physis*) is then brought to perfection by the *techne* of a successor, who may himself start off another new line of development—and it seems highly probable that Xenocrates adopted it from the Peripatetics.

Another source which Pliny used was Duris of Samos, a pupil of Theophrastus. At the beginning of his account of the sculptor

---

[1] See Jex Blake and Sellars, *The Elder Pliny's Chapters on the History of Art*, xvi ff.; Pasquali, *Hermes*, 68 (1913), 162 ff.; B. Schweitzer, *Xenokrates von Athen* (Halle, 1932).

[2] *NH*, xxxiv, 54 (Overbeck, 782).

[3] *NH*, xxxv, 15, 55, 58, 67 (Overbeck, 375, 377, 1075, 1724).

Lysippus Pliny[1] says that according to Duris of Samos Lysippus had no master; he was a bronze-smith and was first fired to try sculpture by a reply of the painter Eupompus, who, when asked what earlier master he followed, pointed to the crowd and said that the artist should imitate nature and not another artist; Lysippus then became a famous sculptor. Three elements in the story agree with the general ideas that we have found in Theophrastus—the genius of the master who has no teacher, the environment which changes his whole life, and the aim of the artist to represent realistically the differences of individual human beings. They translate into the terms of biography the interplay between nature and environment which Theophrastus noted in botany. But this interplay is concentrated into the vivid moment when the young craftsman's whole life was changed by a chance remark of his master. Whether we are entitled to go further and assert that all good-luck stories of self-taught artists derive from Duris and are therefore fictitious does not seem so certain. Duris certainly liked good-luck stories since he tells another of Eumenes and another of Socrates (not the philosopher but the sculptor who became inextricably confused with him),[2] but no doubt good-luck stories were not uncommon. The fact that we can point to a biographical scheme does not prove that the biographies are fictitious. Thus the two strains in art criticism both correspond with the biological views of Theophrastus, the organic growth of the particular art as a result of the interplay of *physis* and *techne* and the biography of the artist seen as the interplay between *physis* and environment.

4. PORTRAITURE

Duris' story of Lysippus is a literary portrait. There are three elements in it: first, as we have said, it describes a decisive interaction between environment and character; secondly, it is vivid

---

[1] *NH*, xxxiv, 61 (Overbeck, 1444); cf. Blake-Sellars, xlviii f. Pfuhl, *MuZ*, para. 748 is much more cautious. On Lysippus cf. above, Ch. III, p. 86 ff.

[2] Plutarch, *Eum.* 1; Diog. Laert. ii, 19.

and exciting and thus brings home the portrait to the reader; thirdly, the event described is unique and only happened to Lysippus. Similarly, Duris recorded the moment which started Eumenes on his career: when he was still a boy, Philip of Macedon came to Cardia and in an idle hour watched the boys' sports; Eumenes was successful and showed both intelligence and courage; Philip therefore took him into his following and his future was assured. This is parallel to the Lysippus story. For vividness of detail we may recall how Duris elaborated Xenophon's simple story of Alcibiades' return into a Hellenistic pageant by giving him not only purple sails but a famous flute-player and a famous actor in full costume to keep his oarsmen in time. This pageant was presumably a fiction, but we have no reason to doubt him when he described the Athenians' flattery of Demetrius of Phalerum and later of Demetrius Poliorcetes. The description extends to the clothes and appearance of the characters.[1] Thus we read that Demetrius Poliorcetes wore boots of purple and gold, a dark-grey cloak embroidered with the golden stars of the firmament and the twelve signs of the Zodiac, and a purple cap tied on by a long band embroidered with gold which floated down to his shoulders, while Demetrius of Phalerum dyed his hair yellow, put rouge on his cheeks, and anointed himself with all kinds of salves, for he wanted to look cheerful and attractive to all who met him. As far as we can see, the portraits drawn by Duris (however prejudiced they may be) are portraits of individuals, just because he tells us of the decisive event which only happened to that character, of the pageants in which he took the leading part, of his individual clothes and personal appearance.

The picturesque detail marks the person out as unlike others, and it is probably this desire to seize the individual which gives early Peripatetic biography its anecdotal character. Beside the biography of individuals we may put the portraits of individuals —the tragic actor in the moment of triumph and weariness after his performance as Achilles, the tragic poet seeking inspiration

[1] Plutarch, *Alc.* 32 (cf. above, Ch. II, p. 21); Ath. 542c; 535e.

from the mask of the young hero, Lycophron contemplating the mask of Cassandra, Demetrius Poliorcetes as a new Poseidon in the glory of military youth, Epicurus at peace after struggling with desire, the mean and pompous Zeno, Crates starting on his travels with his wife, Theophrastus in the lonely, clear-eyed contemplation of research.[1] We may add the haggard, tortured Demosthenes erected in 280 B.C. by Polyeuctus,[2] and the Menander portrait,[3] which was made for the Athenian theatre by Cephisodotus and Timarchus, the sons of the great Praxiteles. We know Menander also from the late Hellenistic relief,[4] which perhaps reproduces a contemporary painting. Inspired by the Muse of Comedy, he composes the speech for a boy in a scene where the boy comes into contact with the mother and father of the girl he loves; the father, so the masks show us, had deserted the mother after raping her and has now returned some seventeen years later to marry her.[5] This is Menander at a particular moment, writing a particular speech in a particular play, which anyone seeing the painting when it was new would be able to name. It is hard to draw the line between these portraits and the portraits discussed in the last chapter. The beginnings of Hellenistic portraiture undoubtedly go back to the time of Alexander. In so far as we can detect a difference it lies in a rather greater emphasis on the particularity of the moment and the subject. Euripides holds the mask of Heracles in one hand and the text of the play in the other, but Menander is depicted as he actually composes a particular speech. The faces and clothes are even more individualised now than in the preceding period; something of the old harsh realism of the early Platonic period appears in the gaunt Demosthenes and the hard lines of his himation, which is as individual

---

[1] Rome, Torlonia, 29. Schefold, *Bildnisse*, 98, 208.

[2] Cf. above, Ch. III, p. 100.

[3] Venice, etc. Schefold, *op. cit.*, 114; Körte, *RE*, s.v. Menandros, 713; Pausanias, i, 21, 1 (Overbeck, 1338) with inscription, Overbeck, 1337.

[4] Rome, Lateran. Pickard-Cambridge, *Festivals*, fig. 93; Bieber, *HT*, fig. 223; *Festschrift für A. Rumpf*, 14 f.; Schefold, *op. cit.*, 165/3; *Greek Theatre Production*, no. C49.   [5] Cf. Webster, *Rylands Bulletin*, 29 (1949), 108 = 15 of the offprint.

in its way as the cosmic cloak of Demetrius Poliorcetes. It would be absurd to suggest that this difference from the preceding period can always be observed; the history of art is much too complicated to be forced into any such simple scheme, but representation of the individual in his external appearance seems to me to be the essential characteristic of portraiture in the late fourth and early third century.

Menander was the pupil of Theophrastus and his portrait in the theatre was made by the sons of Praxiteles. Theophrastus in his will[1] says that he has paid Praxiteles for a statue of Aristotle's son Nicomachus which is to be erected in the Lyceum. This Praxiteles must presumably be a grandson of the great Praxiteles. Is it too bold to suppose that Theophrastus and Menander found in the gentle, sweet art of this family the reflection of their own view of life in general and of individuals in particular? Perhaps we should be wiser to say that it is a dominant Athenian style, inherited from the great Praxiteles' remote but lovely gods and now used also for ordinary mortals, since it was this school that provided the originals for the enchanting Tanagra figures, which begin in the last quarter of the fourth century. The same style can be seen in such sculptures as the ladies from Herculaneum and on the best of contemporary vases such as the assembly of Eleusinian deities on a hydria at Lyons.[2] We may quote of these descendants of Praxitelean art what Sir John Beazley writes of Praxiteles himself: 'the art of Praxiteles mirrors the life of Athens in his time, or at least the life of many Athenians: an intelligent life, quiet-tempered, fond of pleasure and tasteful in its pleasures, taking things lightly, or as lightly as one can.'

Another kind of portraiture is found in Theophrastus' *Characters*. The title of this work was *Ethikoi Charakteres*, which means

---

[1] Diogenes Laertius, v, 52.

[2] Tanagra statuettes: e.g. my *Greek Terracottas*, pls. 4, 5, 36–43; ladies from Herculaneum, Dresden, 326, Winter, *KiB*, 394/1. Athens, Süsserott, *Griechische Plastik des IVten Jahrhunderts*, pl. 37/2. Hydria at Lyons, above, Ch. III, p. 80, n. 1. Beazley and Ashmole, *Greek Sculpture and Painting*, 55.

something like 'Marks of Quality'. Theophrastus could have collected examples of, let us say, 'mean' behaviour and put them together in a chapter entitled 'meanness' without thereby creating a portrait of a 'mean' man. But nowhere in the *Characters* can we say that Theophrastus has introduced instances of behaviour which belong to men of different age or social status, and therefore could not coexist in a single man. At first sight it is surprising that the 'reckless man' is innkeeper, brothelkeeper, gambling-house keeper, butcher, tax-collector, and auctioneer, but the first four obviously go together in the ancient world, and tax-collecting and auctioneering are part-time occupations; a brothelkeeper who is also a tax-collector we know from Comedy.[1] Whether therefore the particular Character consists of a minimum of scenes drawn in detail like the 'coward' or a maximum number of independent acts like the 'reckless' man, they are portraits.

The elements which make up the portraits can be grouped under headings such as personal appearance, religion, life at home, visiting and entertaining friends, life in the market-place, and public life. Often we can see that the portraits are carefully related to each other. First, personal appearance: clothes are the most interesting here, although Theophrastus also describes haircuts, nails, and voices; the oligarch has his himation beautifully draped, the 'complaisant' man has many fine himatia, the man of petty ambition wears a shining himation when he announces a sacrifice, the 'penurious' man wears the smallest possible himation, the 'mean' man only wears a *tribon*, the 'offensive' man wears a thick *chitoniskos* and a very thin stained himation; the 'boor' habitually and the 'gross' man wilfully pull up their clothes indecently high (so that they would look like the actors of Middle Comedy). In one detail, the upkeep of clothes, they seem to be very carefully graded; cleaners are mentioned four times—the 'penurious' man insists on a copious use of fuller's earth so that his himation may

---

[1] Theophrastus, *Char.* 6, 5 (I have taken throughout the English names given by Jebb); cf. Schroeder, *Novae Comoediae Fragmenta*, 3; Page, *Greek Literary Papyri*, no. 66.

keep clean longer; the 'distrustful' man does not choose the best cleaner but the cleaner who can provide the best surety; the 'mean' man stays at home while his himation is being cleaned; and the 'avaricious' man borrows someone else's and goes on wearing it till he is asked to return it.

The few references to religion are worth mentioning because we know that Theophrastus wrote on *Piety* and that his general approach was that god loves the simple sacrifice and regards rather the character of the giver than the magnitude of the gift.[1] In the *Characters*, as would be expected, only deviations occur. The 'superstitious' man exaggerates all religious performances because he is terrified of the gods. The 'late-learner' finds in a sacrifice and an initiation opportunities to show off his late-acquired physical training. The 'offensive' man scratches himself during a sacrifice, swears when his mother comes out of the augur's house and drops the cup during a libation. The 'surly' man refuses to pray when other people pray. The 'mean' man keeps his children from school when there is a feast of the Muses so that they may not have to subscribe, and the 'avaricious' man keeps his children at home for the whole month of Anthesterion when there are many religious ceremonies and therefore they would not get instructional value for his monthly payment. The man of petty ambition cleans, wreathes, and perfumes every day the bronze ring (or finger) that he has dedicated to Asclepius: like the 'late-learner' he finds that religion provides him with an occasion to show off.

If we look at the way in which different characters behave to their wives, we find that the 'penurious' man searches the whole house if his wife has lost a farthing, the 'distrustful' man does not believe his wife when she says that she has locked up, the 'mean' man controls his wife's dowry and does not allow her a maid of her own but hires a servant to go out with her; this is a scale of increasing meanness.

The heading 'visiting and entertaining friends' covers three

---

[1] Cf. the passages from *de Pietate* in Porphyry, *de Abstinentia*, ii, 5–20 (Bernays, *op. cit.*).

F

main types of entertainment: the subscription party, the feast to deme or phratry, the private party given after a sacrifice. At the subscription party the 'penurious' man counts the number of cups that each man drinks and pours the minimum libation, the 'officious' man has more wine mixed than is necessary, the 'avaricious' man gives himself a double portion when carving, and when host charges up fuel, condiments, and lamp oil to the sub-scribers: the 'late-learner' has a party of his contemporaries as if they were young men. When giving a feast, the 'penurious' man cuts the meat up small, the 'avaricious' man does not buy enough bread, feeds his own slaves from the common pot, and inventories the remains. Private entertainment introduces a wider range of characters. After a sacrifice (to celebrate a wedding or some public festival) a party to friends was normal: the 'shameless' man salts the meat for future consumption and dines with someone else, the 'mean' man at his daughter's marriage sells all the meat except for what the priests require; the 'unseasonable' man arrives in the middle of the sacrifice to demand his interest. The 'arrogant' man, before starting for a party, sends someone to announce his com-ing, and the 'flatterer' is ready to perform this service. The 'arro-gant' man does not trouble to appear at his own parties; but the man of petty ambition insists on sitting beside his host. When they arrive the 'flatterer' has presents for the children, the 'com-plaisant' man plays with them and lets them sleep on his knee. In conversation, the 'flatterer' pays continual compliments and attentions to his host, the 'unseasonable' man curses the female sex at a wedding party; the 'loquacious' man talks so much that no one can eat, whereas the 'newsmaker' misses his dinner because he is still telling lies in the market-place; the 'offensive' man belches while he drinks and spits at the cupbearer; the 'unpleasant' man as guest describes the workings of his own inside and praises the water from his well, the vegetables from his garden, and the skill of his cook. At the musical stage of the party the 'surly' man refuses to sing or recite or dance, the 'late-learner' breaks down in his recitation, the 'reckless' man dances the kordax without being drunk, the 'unseasonable' man catches hold of a guest who is still sober to support him after his dance. Similar comparisons can be made of conduct in the theatre, gymnasium, and agora, but enough has been said to show how in each sphere of life the characters are related to one another.

We can also see coincidences and contrasts in the performance of the same action by different characters: the 'avaricious man' and the 'shameless man' both borrow minor household goods such as salt from their neighbours; the 'avaricious man' merely wants to get something for nothing, the 'shameless man' takes an additional pleasure in making the lender carry the stuff home for him: the 'thrifty man' refuses to lend such things because he dislikes the most trivial loss, but the 'suspicious man' refuses to lend because he does not trust his neighbour.

The portraits were therefore composed with reference to each other. Whether the gallery is complete is difficult to say, but it would probably be unwise to infer that it is not from the single late reference[1] to a 'brave man' as a foil to the coward. To say that all the portraits are of bad men would be untrue, because there is no malice and little ridicule in this sympathetic record of their behaviour, but it is true to say that all except two (the 'stupid' and the 'superstitious' man) are demonstrably related to the list of excesses and defects in Aristotle's *Ethics*. Theophrastus' procedure (as has recently been made clear by D. J. Furley)[2] is the reverse of Aristotle's. Aristotle notes the behaviour of men in order to establish a definition of a particular virtue or its corresponding excess or defect; Theophrastus starts from the definition and records the behaviour of the man who corresponds to it. But there is a further point. We have noticed already in Theophrastus' botany his insistence on minor subdivisions rather than broad general categories, and in ethics we know that he distinguished *mempsis*, *orge*, and *thymos* (?criticism, sudden rage, and fierce temper) as distinct passions.[3] So here developing hints in Aristotle, Theophrastus subdivides 'meanness' into 'penuriousness',

[1] Eustathius on *Iliad*, 13, 276. [2] *Symbolae Osloenses*, 30 (1953), 56. [3] fr. 72.

'recklessness', and 'avariciousness'. Aristotle's 'vain' man is sub-divided into the 'arrogant' man, the man of petty ambition, and the grumbler. The oligarch and the patron of rascals are special instances of the 'ambitious' man who seeks the wrong sort of honour. Theophrastus has greatly increased the number of social sinners: the 'evil-speaker', the 'unreasonable', the 'unpleasant' and the 'distrustful' are new versions of Aristotelian 'churlishness'; the 'officious', the 'newsmaker', the 'loquacious' man, and the 'garrulous' man are variations of the 'boaster'. The 'boor' of Aristotle is subdivided into the 'boor', the 'offensive' man, and the 'late-learner'.

We have then a gallery of thirty portraits composed with reference to each other. After the preliminary definition nothing is given except observable details. Aristotle, as we have seen, sometimes recorded these in his process of defining virtues and vices, but Theophrastus has made the same kind of details—performance of liturgies, entertainment of guests, behaviour to strangers, conversation, voice, gestures, and dress—not only a system by which one character can be compared with another but also the whole content of his portraits. No more complete realisation of Lysippus' claim to represent men 'as they appear' could be imagined, and thus Theophrastus' procedure is in line with Hellenistic portraiture.

Theophrastus did not write his *Characters* to establish ethical definitions but rather to give examples of the defined qualities as they could be observed in everyday life. We know four possible practical uses for such a work. The *Auctor ad Herennium*[1] wrote a character sketch of 'a braggart' which is worthy of Theophrastus; he calls the process *notatio*, the description of a character by clear signs which are attributed to it like marks (*notae*). Here we have the Characters used by the orator as a weapon for the court, and there is undoubtedly a Greek tradition behind this, which can be traced back to Aristotle's remark in the *Rhetoric*[2] that the narrative of a speech must show *ethos*: 'e.g. that he talked while he

[1] iv, 50, 63.   [2] *Rhet.* 1417 a 22.

walked: for this shows boorishness of character.' Secondly, Theophrastus' 'affable man' is quoted by Philodemus[1] in a passage deriving from Ariston of Keos, which describes particular vices and their consequences and then prescribes remedies. This clearly belongs to Ethics. Thirdly, in Menander's *Second Adelphoi*[2] Micio justifies his treatment of his adopted son by saying: 'There are many signs in a man which make it easy and possible to say, when two people do the same thing, "this will not harm the one but will harm the other", not because the act differs but because the agent differs.' The *Characters* were written some twenty-five years before the *Second Adelphoi* and describe just such *signa in homine* which reveal a man's quality; we are reminded of the 'penurious' man and the 'suspicious' man, who refuse to lend their household goods for quite different reasons. Thus the *Characters* could be used as an educational handbook both by the educator (like Micio), who wants to assess his pupil, and by the educator, like his brother Demea[3] in the same play, who wants to provide his pupil with examples to avoid. The writer of the prologue, whether Theophrastus himself or a later editor, saw it in the latter sense: 'our sons will be better if they have such records which they can use as examples.'

5. COMEDY

Unless we can accept the prologue as genuine, we cannot say which, if any, of these three objects Theophrastus had in mind. We can however be certain that the *Characters* was not designed as a source book for drawing characters in comedy, as has been suggested. About a third of the portraits have nothing to do with comedy at all, and of the rest those which we expect to be most like comedy because comic characters of the same name are recognisable long before Theophrastus, show striking divergencies. The flatterer, the braggart, and the boor are all coloured by

---

[1] In Philodemus, *on Vices*, x. cf. Regenbogen, *op. cit.*, 1507.
[2] Terence, *Ad.* 821.   [3] Terence, *Ad.* 415.

comedy, but the flatterer is neither a parasite nor an intriguer as he is in comedy. The braggart is neither a soldier nor a wise man nor a cook as he is in comedy, and some of the traits of the comic 'braggart' belong to Theophrastus' 'arrogant' man. The boor also has not the violence of the old comic countryman nor his habit of misbehaving at parties when he is persuaded to join them; that trait belongs to Theophrastus' 'late-learner'. The *Characters* both draw from Comedy and give to Comedy but they were not written to help comic poets; if they had been, they would have been much more like the comic characters we know and the super-fluity of fathers would have been balanced by sons and women.

If the *Characters* were published in or soon after 319, as a good deal of evidence suggests,[1] Theophrastus was writing them while Menander was his pupil and during the years that he was pro-ducing his first plays. It is therefore perfectly natural that the men in Menander's plays should occasionally echo Theophrastus' *Characters*. Euclio in the *Aulularia*,[2] like Theophrastus' 'penu-rious' man, goes to the market and comes back without buying anything and refuses to lend minor household goods, and Gnatho in the *Kolax*,[3] like Theophrastus' 'flatterer', 'laughs at flat jokes' and 'cannot contain his laughter'. But Gnatho is here only playing a part to help his friend—a trait which has no place in Theo-phrastus' flatterer; and Menander's Boor (or Rustic) in the play named after him is not a boorish old man but a boy who has been brought up in the country and runs wild when he comes to town.

Far more important than occasional cross-references between the plays and Theophrastus' *Characters* is the general influence of Peripatetic philosophy on Menander and through him on Apollo-dorus of Carystus, an influence less strongly felt by the rather older comic poets Philemon and Diphilus, although they too show it in some degree. This influence can be seen in masks and costumes,

---

[1] Newsmaker and Braggart have references to events of 319 (see Leipzig edition). Oligarch, Patron of rascals, Evil-speaker, Loquacious man, and Mean man all show signs of having been composed between 325 and 316.

[2] Plautus, *Aul.* 371 f., 95 f.   [3] Terence, *Eun.* 421, 497.

language, structure, character-drawing, and the general conception of comedy. We cannot completely untangle the influence of
classical tragedy from the influence of philosophy, since classical
tragedy influenced Menander both directly and through the
medium of Peripatetic philosophy. As serious drama seen on the
stage year after year, classical tragedy was both a source of situations and an example of technique in handling dramatic problems
and a repository of wisdom (like Shakespeare) which characters
could quote in the knowledge that they would be understood by
the audience, but it was also the foundation of Peripatetic theory
of drama, and at the same time provided the philosophers with
recognisable examples of ethical and unethical behaviour. Thus
when tragedy had practically ceased to be a live art, classical
tragedy of the fifth century, directly in the theatre and indirectly
through the philosophers, became the inspiration of New Comedy,
which was now the only live drama in Athens and was redressed
to suit its new seriousness.

Probably the break between Middle Comedy and New Comedy
appears much sharper than it actually was, since we are apt to
think only of Aristophanes and Menander. In the preceding
chapter I have tried to say something of the development of the
Comedy of intrigue and recognition in the third quarter of the
fourth century, and noted the gradual introduction of new masks
as new types of character were needed. It is also clear that much
traditional comedy survived: even the papyri throw up an occasional obscene word which produces from the editors a shocked
comment 'this cannot be Menander'; and the climax of the *Casina*
(for which a parallel in Old Comedy can be provided) is sometimes ascribed to Plautus rather than to Diphilus. Moreover the
slaves' masks and the old women's masks remained distorted
caricatures as they had been through the whole history of Comedy.
Nevertheless there is a break:[1] new and much more comely masks
are introduced for old men and young men; the actors are no
longer padded in front and behind; the phallus is seldom visible;

[1] Cf. *Studies in Later Greek Comedy*, 119 f.

in fact the characters appear like the ordinary everyday Athenian. These changes had a double significance; first, the characters of comedy looked like members of ordinary upper-class households, and secondly more masks were available, particularly for old men, young men, and young women, so that their appearance gave more indication of their character. The break is partly due to changed circumstances, but partly, I suspect, to Menander himself. Menander's first production was in 321, and thus (except for the brief break between 319 and 317) the first fourteen years of his production fell in the period of restricted franchise; it is probable that during these years free tickets at the theatre were abolished, and certain that the rich counted for more in the state than before; the people who appear in Theophrastus' *Characters* are the people who formed the older part of the audience of New Comedy[1] and among them unseemliness is rare and noted with some disapproval. In the portrait-relief of which we have already spoken Menander has two of the new masks and it seems likely that the new costume came in with the new masks, but we have, as far as I know, no positive evidence to date the new costume before the early third century.

New Comedy was one of the most fruitful art forms that the Athenians produced, and was exported all over the Hellenistic world, nor is its influence yet dead in the theatre, as the *Confidential Clerk* shows. Each of the three great writers of whom we can form some idea had his own aims and each felt the influence of philosophy in a rather different way. Menander in the *Perikeiromene*,[2] produced in 313 or very soon after, tells the story of a pair of lovers, a soldier Polemon and an orphan Glykera. Polemon comes back from the war and is told by his soldier servant that he has seen Glykera embracing an unknown young man; Polemon calls Glykera out, cuts off her hair with his sword and then goes off to drown his sorrows with an elderly friend Pataikos. This is

---

[1] Most of the Characters have slaves, and slave-owners according to A. H. M. Jones (*Past and Present*, i, 20) only represented about a quarter of the citizen population.   [2] Cf. *Studies in Menander*, 5 f.

the first scene; then personified Ignorance, *Agnoia*, comes on and tells the audience the background of the story including the essential fact that the unknown young man is Glykera's brother: 'All this blazed up for the sake of the future, that Polemon might fly into a rage—for I, Ignorance, led him, though his character is not such—that a beginning of revelation might be made and that they might discover their own.'

Ignorance is a personification of a mental state; we have seen many such during our survey of fourth-century art and literature but this figure has a direct connection with Peripatetic philosophy. The speech has been described as a sermon on an Aristotelian text. Polemon's ignorance makes his action in cutting off Glykera's hair what Aristotle defines as a 'misfortune' and not culpable. An act done in a rage or intoxication is not a misfortune and is culpable, but is still less blameworthy than a premeditated injustice. Menander called two of his earliest plays *Rage (Orge)* and *Intoxication (Methe)*, and it seems probable that they were the prologue figures of those plays. A rather different prologue figure is Boetheia, translated by Plautus as *Auxilium*, who spoke the prologue of the *Synaristosai*;[1] Boetheia is assistance to an injured innocent —here the girl who had been abandoned in her youth and is in the course of the play restored to her parents so that her liaison with her lover may be converted into legitimate marriage.

The largest composition of figures of this kind is Apelles' picture of Slander which is described by Lucian.[2] A man with large ears is seated between two women, Ignorance and False Assumption. He holds out a hand to greet Slander, a beautiful but frenzied-looking woman, who has a torch in her left hand and with her right drags along by the hair a young man who raises his hands to heaven and invokes the testimony of the gods. Ahead of her walks Jealousy, a pale, ugly man with sharp eyes, who seems wasted away by disease. She is also accompanied by Plotting and Deception. Behind her Repentance, a weeping woman in black

---

[1] Cf. *Studies in Menander*, 91, 208.
[2] Lucian, *Cal. non tem. cred.*, 4 (Overbeck, 1874).

tattered clothes, looks back at Truth, who forms the end of the procession. Whether the picture was or was not occasioned by a personal experience of Apelles does not matter. The story is clear enough: a man listens to slander because he is ignorant of the facts and ready to make false assumptions; the slander is due to the jealousy of the second man, who is led thereby to plotting and deception. The whole picture shows successive psychological states of the two men, and Slander, Jealousy and Repentance at least are characterised so as to be at once recognisable. We need not say that we can see the influence of Aristotle, but we are at least justified in noting that Apelles was a younger contemporary of Aristotle and probably an exact contemporary of Theophrastus.

Menander also followed Aristotle in the nice discrimination of motives, like Theophrastus when he distinguished between criticism, sudden rage, and fierce temper. This appears again in the scene where Polemon, having tried to regain Glykera by force, asks his older friend Pataikos to use persuasion: Pataikos points out that as Glykera is not legally married to him, she is her own mistress and can leave him if she chooses and he has no right to take summary vengeance on her supposed lover. Glykera refuses to forgive him for treating her 'as one would not treat any slave girl', until she finds that she is not a kept orphan but Pataikos' daughter; then she allows her father to give her to him in marriage. The recognition scene is necessary to put Glykera in a position where she can forgive. The characters are treated with great sympathy and stand out as individuals: Glykera in her heroism and unselfishness, Polemon in his passionate jealous love, the irresponsible young brother Moschion, and the rather pathetically experienced Pataikos, who had exposed his children because he lost his fortune and his wife on successive days.

As far as was possible on the Greek stage, the characters of New Comedy were individualised in appearance. If standard masks did not allow individualism to go far, at least the main figures wore ordinary clothes and were not caricatured. The fact that competent archaeologists can debate whether a Hellenistic mask is comic or tragic and whether a Hellenistic statuette represents a father of comedy or is a portrait of a philosopher is some evidence of this. In language Menander (and probably his contemporaries went with him) broke with the comic convention of uniformly extravagant speech and only retained metre to mark their words off from ordinary conversation. Körte[1] says: 'More than any earlier dramatist Menander has adapted the language to each particular person: the slave talks differently from the master, the old man from the youth, and the wife from the nurse or the hetaira.' This is well illustrated in the sequence of scenes in the *Epitrepontes* (532 ff.), where the *hetaira* Habrotonon shows Charisios' wife, Pamphile, the baby which she had exposed, then the slave Onesimos describes Charisios' reaction to his wife's refusal to leave him when she believed him unfaithful, and finally we see Charisios himself:

HABROTONON: I'll go out with the baby. It's been crying some time, poor little thing. I don't know what I've done wrong with it.

PAMPHILE: If only the gods would be kind to me!

HABROTONON: My darling baby, you'll see mother. She's coming just when we want her.

PAMPHILE: I'll go.

HABROTONON: Lady, wait a moment.

PAMPHILE: Are you speaking to me?

HABROTONON: Yes. Look and see if you recognise me, lady. It is the girl I saw. How do you do, my dear?

PAMPHILE: But who are you?

HABROTONON: Give me your hand. Tell me, darling, did you come last year to see the Tauropolia in a silk gown?

PAMPHILE: Lady, where did you get, tell me, the child you are carrying?

[1] *RE*, s.v. Menandros, 702.

HABROTONON: Do you see something you recognise, my dear, among his things? Don't be afraid of me, lady.

PAMPHILE: You aren't its mother?

HABROTONON: No, I pretended to be, not to hurt its mother but to find her at my leisure. Now I have found her. For it was you I saw then.

PAMPHILE: But who is the father?

HABROTONON: Charisios.

PAMPHILE: My dear, do you know that for certain?

HABROTONON: Yes, for certain. But aren't you the wife from this house?

PAMPHILE: Yes.

HABROTONON: You lucky woman, the gods have been kind to you. But there's a noise at the door; someone's coming out from the next house. Take me in with you so that you can hear all the rest.

[*Exeunt into* CHARISIOS' *house.*]

[*Enter* ONESIMOS *from* CHAERESTRATOS' *house.*]

ONESIMOS: He's mad, by Apollo, stark, staring, raving mad, by the gods. I mean my master, Charisios. Black bile has got into him or some such thing. What other explanation can there be? A little time ago he spent ever so long bending down and listening through the keyhole. His wife's father was talking to her about the business apparently. The way Charisios changed colour was too horrible for words. And he shouted out, 'My darling, how nobly you speak', and he beat his head hard with his hands. Then after a pause, 'What a noble wife I had and how miserably I have lost her.' Finally when he had heard all and come in—roaring, tearing of the hair, frenzy! 'I'm the sinner,' he kept saying. 'I had done the same thing myself and become the father of a bastard, but I hadn't a shred of mercy for her when she was in the same misfortune, pitiless barbarian that I am.' He kept cursing himself: his eyes were bloodshot and his face purple. I'm frightened, I'm stiff with fear. For in this state, if he sees me he might kill me because I told him the story. Therefore I have slipped out here. And where am I to turn? to what plan? I'm done, I'm lost. There's a noise; he's coming out. Saviour Zeus, if it is possible, save me.

[*Exit into* CHARISIOS' *house.*]

[*Enter* CHARISIOS *from* CHAERESTRATOS' *house.*]

CHARISIOS: I so faultless, looking to repute and considering what is honour and what disgrace, so pure, so irreproachable in my life. God has used me well and fittingly. Here I've shown that I am only a man. You unhappy wretch, you talk so loud and proud? You cannot bear a woman's unwilling mischance. I'll show that you've committed a like sin. And she'll be kind to you then, but you dishonour her. You'll be shown a man unfortunate and foolish and unwise. Her words to her father were very like your thoughts then, weren't they? She said she had come to share your life and therefore must not run away from the mischance that had befallen. But you in your loftiness . . . Her father will be most hasty with her. What do I care for her father? I'll say right out: 'Don't bother me, Smikrines. My wife is not leaving me. Why do you fuss and nag at Pamphile?'

[*Enter* ONESIMOS *and* HABROTONON *from* CHARISIOS' *house.*]

Habrotonon is a harpist and a slave, who desires above all things else to gain her freedom. She hoped to do it by making Charisios fall in love with her, but he would have nothing to do with her and so she tries and succeeds by finding the parents of the baby. Her care for the baby and her sympathy with Pamphile are obvious. The distinction between the two women is subtly marked by the vocatives. Habrotonon is a little too affectionate. She advances from the formal 'lady' to 'my dear' and 'darling' before Pamphile has recognised her, but is sensitive enough to return to 'lady' when Pamphile draws back, as she thinks; she is good-hearted as well as shrewd. Pamphile is only seen for a moment, and what was probably her great scene, the scene with her father, is lost. But even so she makes a clear impression. From the fragments of her scene with her father and from Charisios' account of it in our passage it is clear that Smikrines spared her nothing in describing his view of the relations between Charisios and Habrotonon, whom he believes to be the mother of the child. There is a reminiscence of Sophocles' Deianira and Euripides' Andromache in her answer: 'I have come to share his life and must not run away from the mischance that has befallen.' She chooses unhesitatingly between the easy course of returning home to a father who knows nothing of her own mischance and the harder way of continuing in the house of a husband who has left her and, as it now appears, has long been unfaithful to her. In the depths of her misery she meets Habrotonon and faces her with admirable reserve until she recognises the child's trinkets. In calling Charisios' act a mischance, she is more generous than Habrotonon who calls it an 'injustice' (323).

Onesimos' account of Charisios' behaviour when he overheard Pamphile's conversation with her father completes the picture of Charisios, which has been built up by the earlier descriptions of Smikrines, Onesimos, Habrotonon (and probably also Chaerestratos) and prepares us for his appearance. It is also characteristic of the slave not only in its sentiments but also in its language—the variants of μαίνεσθαι at the beginning, the string of abstracts like a doctor's prescription 'roaring, tearing of hair, frenzy', the staccato phrasing of the end.

Charisios himself has something of the priggishness of Euripides' Hippolytus and therefore many of the lines in his monologue have the ring of tragic iambics: e.g. 'a man unfortunate and foolish and unwise'. His line 'so pure, so irreproachable in my life' is borrowed from the description of the upright man from the country in Euripides' Orestes (922), and Charisios means to make this comparison between the simple morality of the countryman and his own philosophy which did not prevent him from doing wrong.

Here at the end of our period we have sympathetic portraiture of individuals, which is expressed in the observable details of appearance, speech, and behaviour. Comedy now deals, as Theophrastus says, with 'private affairs'.[1] The chance preservation of Menander enables us to assess his art with more precision than that of the other comic poets to whom we can now turn.

The play by Diphilus which Plautus translated as the *Rudens*[2] also has a prologue figure, Arcturus, the star which not only causes the shipwreck but also acts as a recording angel to report human transgressions to Zeus, a function already given to the stars in Plato's *Epinomis*.[3] Personification of the stars was long established, but the astronomical advances of the fourth century gave them new life and a new sanction. So we expect that the guilty will suffer and the virtuous be rewarded. In this play the good and the bad are clearly divided; the old man Daemones, the priestess, the young man Plesidippus, his slave Trachalio, and the two girls are good, the *leno* and his friend, the slave Sceparnio, and the fisherman Gripus are bad. There are none of the finer shades which make Polemon in the *Perikeiromene* partly good and partly bad, and there is no reason to suppose that Plautus missed them, since in Euclio in the *Aulularia* he has preserved the shading of Menander. Diphilus does not share Menander's desire to penetrate the conventional colour of a braggart soldier or *hetaira* to the real value beneath. Daemones is the most interesting character in the *Rudens* and he stands for an ideal of conduct which Theophrastus would have appreciated: he has been driven out of Athens because he spent his fortune in helping others (it sounds as if he lost his citizen rights in the restriction of the franchise); in Cyrene he gives of his poverty to all who ask of him; and in his decision against Gripus he shows the nice discrimination of Aristotle's equitable man in deciding cases which are not entirely covered by law. As in Menander, the play constantly reminds us of tragedy, not only of Euripides in many scenes, but also of Sophocles' *Ajax* in the entry of the two girls searching for each other and of the

---

[1] Kaibel, *CGF*, 57.   [2] Cf. *Studies in Later Greek Comedy*, 159 f., 165 f.
[3] Fraenkel, *CQ*, 36 (1942), 12 compares *Epinomis* 984d, cf. on Aristotle, Jaeger, *Aristotle*, 142 ff.; on Xenocrates, Boyancé, *REA*, 50 (1948), 225; on Eudoxus, Schadewaldt, in *Satura Weinreich*, 128 ff.

Aeschylean *Diktyoulkoi* when Gripus fishes up the chest of recognition tokens. The play is full of spectacle both acted and narrated: the startling prologue figure Arcturus, Sceparnio tiling his master's roof after the storm and then describing the shipwreck, the arrival of the two girls, the fishermen discussing their trade, the dialogue of the dripping old villains, Daemones' dream of the monkey and the swallows, the establishment of the two girls on the altar of Aphrodite, the posting of two men with clubs to keep guard on the *leno*, and the arrival of Gripus with his basket. If only Daemones has anything of the subtlety of Menander's character drawing, the play has other merits, the spectacle of which we have spoken and the brilliant interweaving of the two themes of liberation and recognition into a plot which goes forward in well-marked chapters till the wicked are punished and the virtuous rewarded.

Philemon's *Thesauros*,[1] Plautus' *Trinummus*, begins with two prologue figures, Luxury and Poverty. Luxury sends her daughter Poverty into the house of the young man who has spent all his money on luxurious living. There are two obvious precedents for these figures, Wealth and Poverty in Aristophanes' *Plutus* and Iris and Lyssa in Euripides' *Hercules Furens*. They are persuasive personifications of the kind that go back ultimately to Homer's Ate; by this period the Cynics[2] were particularly fond of such ethical personifications, and the Stoic Cleanthes[3] has left a fragment of a dialogue in which Reason asks Passion what it wants. Their presence in Philemon is a kind of advertisement that this is a solemn play about a rake's progress. The play is full of moralising, particularly the opening soliloquy by the good young man on the contrast between the life of love and the life of ambition, and the long discussion of the character of the bad young man by the good young man and his father. But the moralising is not particularly in character and is much lengthier than the occasion

---

[1] *Studies in Later Greek Comedy*, 140 f.
[2] e.g. Crates 2 and 7 Diehl; Bion, 4, 6; Demetrius ap. Stob., viii 20.
[3] fr. 570 von Arnim, 7 Powell.

demands. It seems rather to be superadded to meet the taste of an audience educated by Menander than to arise from Philemon's conception of comedy.

The real Philemon is seen better in the *Mercator* (*Emporos*) and *Mostellaria* (*Phasma*). No one could write a better comic sequence than the series of scenes in the *Phasma* from the arrival of the slave Tranio with the news that the young man's father has arrived. The young man is having a party with his girl and a friend; the friend is very drunk and Tranio has some difficulty in driving the revellers into the house before the father arrives. Then the father has to be frightened away from his own house; Tranio invents the story that the house is haunted by the ghost which gives the play its name. Then Tranio is faced with both the moneylender (who had provided the money for the son to buy his girl) and the father; he has the brilliant idea of telling the father that the money was borrowed to pay for a new house. The father wants to see it, and Tranio has to persuade the neighbour to show his house, and at the same time prevent the father from asking awkward questions. These are admirable scenes in which Tranio is driven from one rash position to another, and this is the kind of comedy in which Philemon excels. It has no serious intention and is none the worse for that; when Philemon is serious he is dull.

6. CONCLUSION

Even through the Latin translations we can appreciate the differences between the three great comic poets of the late fourth century. Their similarities are however for our present purpose more important than their differences. Philemon seems to us perhaps more akin to Middle Comedy than the other two, and yet if we are right in supposing the *Persa* and the *Menaechmi* to be adaptations of Middle Comedy, Philemon's characters are developed in much more detail than any that we know in Middle Comedy. The formula is essentially the same: a man of such and such a kind will behave in such and such a way in such and such a situation. But the situation, though sometimes extravagant, is nearer ordinary life than before and the characters (or at least some of them) awake sympathy as well as laughter. Theophrastus' definition of Comedy as 'private affairs' or 'events of ordinary life' is a good general heading for much art and literature of the late fourth and early third century. He himself gives the theory behind it in his botany when he describes the influence of environment and the linking of things together. The individual is interesting because he is unique and yet he is closely linked to many others. So in Menander particularly the boundaries between the types of character are not so hard as we expect, and Polemon in the *Perikeiromene* or Thais in the *Eunuch* take on quite a new aspect. The Hellenistic philosophies are directed to solving the problems of everyday life and Hellenistic portraiture is concerned with its observable details. Surrounded and sometimes harmed, sometimes helped by those flamboyant figures the successors of Alexander, Athenian society goes on, represented sympathetically in art by the descendants of Praxiteles and in literature by Menander, who seems to have believed, like Theophrastus, that everything has an instinct for good.

Just before he died in 262, Philemon saw in a dream nine girls leaving his house. They were the nine Muses and the story is a pretty variant on the theme that a god or goddess may not watch a mortal die. But we may think of it also as symbolic of the spread of Athenian culture over the Hellenistic world and remember that twenty years later Greek Comedy was being produced in Rome.

V

Conclusion

ATHENS was a small city, too small for the philosopher to live
in isolation from the writer or the artist or for the artist
and the writer to be ignorant of the philosopher. We
should think in terms of Oxford or Cambridge rather than of
London, but of an Oxford or Cambridge which produced creative
artists as well as academics and was the artistic and intellectual
centre of the world. In such a town, particularly under ancient
conditions, poets, artists, and thinkers must have met continually,
and in the preceding pages I have tried to give some account of
their interaction. If we ask what is the evidence for this interaction,
I suppose that we should think first of the knowledge that Plato
and Aristotle (and Theophrastus, though to a smaller degree,
because less of him survives) show of art and literature. Plato not
only criticises painting but knows its technical processes; Aristotle
mentions Theodectes and Astydamas by the side of Sophocles.
We should think also of the presence of Aristophanes, the doctor
Eryximachus, and Alcibiades as well as Socrates at Agathon's
celebration in the *Symposium* or of the party at Cephalus' house
which is the setting of the *Republic*; there is no reason to suppose
that such gatherings were not still held in the fourth century, to
which period their recording belongs. Or we may think of the
relationship of the tragedian Theodectes with the orator Isocrates
and the philosopher Aristotle.

Theodectes came from Phaselis in Lycia, and so provides evidence for my second statement that Athens was the intellectual

and artistic capital of the Greek world. This statement implies both that Athens was the centre and that communications were good. We need only remember the variety of nationalities represented in the Academy, Aristotle from Stageira, Theophrastus from Eresus, Eudoxus from Cnidus, the Sicilian doctor and the Chaldaean. Plato himself says that a tragic poet must win his spurs in Athens, and the list of comic poets who succeeded in Athens includes Amphis from Euboea, Alexis from Thurii, Philemon from Syracuse, and Diphilus from Sinope. The same is true of artists. The sculptor of the Demeter of Cnidus also carved an Alexander for the Athenian Acropolis. Lysippus, himself a Sicyonian, made works at Athens, Delphi, Dion in Macedonia, Olympia, Tarentum and other places, as well as at Corinth and Sicyon. Athenian vases illustrated in this book were found in N. Africa, S. Russia, Samnium, Sicily, and Etruria as well as Athens.[1] The stylistic links binding the vase-painters of South Italy to the Peloponnese and Athens are many and complicated. Artistically and intellectually the Greek world is united; there are important local centres in the Peloponnese (painting and sculpture), at Syracuse under the elder Dionysius, at Tarentum, and towards the end of our period at Alexandria, but the capital is Athens.

At first sight it seemed doubtful whether a comparative study of the art and literature of the fourth century would yield any results. 'In the fourth century and later the story is more confusing. The chief cause is perhaps the specialisation of the arts. Fourth-century ethical and political thought belongs to the philosophers and not to the poets or artists, and the creative ideas of a generation can no longer be summed up in pairs of names like Aeschylus and Polygnotus or Sophocles and Pheidias. Instead, a number of series survive which have no such obvious cross-connection with each other.' I wrote that in 1944 and it still seems to me to be true. But as I tried to see art and literature in relation to the three great

[1] N. Africa: pl. 11, 5a, 10b. S. Russia: pl. 4b. Sicily: pl. 7. Samnium: pl. 10a. Etruria: pl. 3b, 4a. Athens: pl. 2.

philosophers I became more aware of the cross-connections. These are however of a different kind from the cross-connections observable in the fifth century, where it is justifiable to make detailed formal comparisons between the arts and to apply the terms strong style, classical style, rich style, etc. indifferently to poetry, sculpture, painting, and even prose.

In the fourth century these likenesses of external form are not so apparent, although it is perfectly true that in art it would be possible to trace a sequence of rich style, strong style, free style, and there would be a certain justification in ranging Isocrates, Demosthenes, Dinarchus and even Plato, Aristotle, Theophrastus under the same three headings. It is conceivable that *Rhesus*, Theodectes, Lycophron in tragedy and *Ecclesiazusae*, original of *Persa*, and original of *Miles Gloriosus* could be seen as similar dramatic series. But for the fourth century a division into styles does not seem to me so fruitful as a division into three attitudes, which I call seeing in contrasts, seeing the structure, and seeing the appearance. Before however discussing these three attitudes a little further let us be clear what they are not. They are not three successive and mutually exclusive ways of looking at things. The first way seems to me rather more common in the earlier part of the century but I can find later examples, the second seems to me characteristic of the middle of the century but I could provide earlier and later instances, the third is Hellenistic but not exclusively Hellenistic. At any moment there are men of different ages producing work characteristic of their different generations and at the same moment there are men of the same age who are conservative, radical, and revolutionary. The individual creator does not develop uniformly; he may be tired or elated, he may in the same work include with his newest and best older stuff which is good enough, he may not himself have worked out yet the full implications of his new discovery. All this must be remembered when we apply the three attitudes of mind.

Plato's theory of Forms, Aristotle's statement that nature is not like an episodic tragedy, and Theophrastus' *Characters* are instances of the three attitudes of mind. I do not mean either that these attitudes were invented by the philosophers or that they were imposed by the philosophers on writers or artists. In a comparatively small society the give and take of ideas must have been continuous and we certainly cannot sort out originators now; in that particular kind of atmosphere it is often wrong to speak of an originator at all. There are a few instances where we can suggest priorities. The detached, smiling, young divinities of Praxiteles[1] are the artistic expression of the new philosophical conception of the divine; both conception and expression were probably new in the last third of the fifth century. Euphranor's dignified heroes and the self-restraint of Theodectes' Philoctetes may well be an answer to the criticisms of the *Republic*. I suspect further that Plato's kindlier view of art and literature in his later dialogues was influenced by the Sicyonian school of painting and by the emphasis on composition in Isocratean rhetoric, and that these in turn made it easier for Aristotle to find in art and literature a parallel for the operations of nature in which he was primarily interested. The rules which he thus formulated in the *Poetics* gave New Comedy the firm structure on which to develop the individual appearances of its characters, portrayed as individuals each in his or her own language. But there must have been far more give and take than we can now appreciate, and we must always remember that Plato and Aristotle overlapped for twenty years and Aristotle and Theophrastus for thirty, so that even the three philosophers cannot always be clearly distinguished from each other.

Seeing in contrasts is an old way of seeing, which can already be remarked in Homer and geometric vases and had entered philosophy very certainly by the time of Parmenides. In the later fifth century both realism and formalism had tended to obscure the clear contrasts of Sophoclean tragedy and the Parthenon frieze. Gorgias, if anyone, expressed himself in contrasts, but their swift alternation gave his prose an all-over pattern, which minimised

[1] Cf. Pl. 6.

their effects. Isocrates loosened this structure by making the elements larger and the contrasts thereby more apparent, but still the effect is rather one of pattern than of contrast. Nevertheless seeing in contrasts is a useful description of much work in the early fourth century. In Lysias the contrast between the family of Cephalus and the Thirty Tyrants is entirely clear. Plato himself sees the Forms in their place beyond heaven contrasted with the sensibles of our world, and this contrast is worked out in more stages in the four sections of the line, the different levels in the Cave, the fish analogy of the *Phaedo* and many other examples. Seeing in contrasted levels was natural to the Greek since the dramatist also had his contrasted levels of gods, actors, and chorus, and the painter similarly disposed his scenes.[1] Plato stresses the contrast between Socrates' uncouth appearance and the golden words he speaks, and this dissonance is repeated by the sculptor of the Lyme Park relief, who opposes the weary disillusioned comic poet to the joyous masks of his creation;[2] in mythological comedy itself the appearance and utterances of the characters contrast with their heroic and divine names. One level of the ascending planes or one term of the contrast, is usually our world and in presenting it we find a very effective realism, which achieves its effect with a maximum of economy.

But in Plato himself the tendency to see the structure is also clear from the first. This too is an inheritance from the classical and early classical period of the fifth century. It is implicit in Socrates' refusal to accept Anaxagoras' use of Nous as a *deus ex machina* and his demand for an explanation of everything in terms of the Good. So in spite of their contrasts the sections of the Line and the levels in the Cave are part of a single ascent to knowledge of the Good, and even the lowest section or level is somehow dependent on the Good. The world of the *Timaeus* is an organic whole designed by a craftsman, and Aristotle's world is like a work of art made by *Physis*. This principle of organic unity is far reaching in its application. It is a standard to which to create and by

[1] Cf. Pl. 4*b*.   [2] Pl. 1.

which to criticise literature and art. In art the Sicyonian school led
the way both in painting and in sculpture: the Apoxyomenus of
Lysippus and the Alexander mosaic[1] (whether from an original
by a Sicyonian painter or not) are outstanding examples. There is
however a further point: in art and literature the organic unity is
designed to have an effect on the spectator. Both in the *Phaedrus*
and in the *Poetics* the theory is closely connected with the emotional effect to be created in the audience; the origin of this application lies, I have suggested, with Isocrates and Theodectes. It is
reasonable to suppose that Theodectes' tragedies were organically
composed to have the maximum emotional effect, and Aristotle
attests the good structure of late Middle Comedy, for which we
have some evidence in Plautus' *Persa*. The spectator of Euphranor's pictures must have been drawn into the scene by the magnificent figures which face him like giants from their restricting
frames, and must have shared the emotion welling from their
sunken eyes. The gods of the Eleusinian scenes[2] are anything but
detached spectators and swept their audience into the emotional
release of the mysteries. The jury or the assembly vibrated to the
passion of Demosthenes' inevitably constructed periods. The
same organic prose, only more finely drawn and nervous, expresses Aristotle's own thought. Organic structure is the principle
of his dealings with the natural world, and he transferred the concept to explain the history of poetry and art, thus laying the foun-
dations of historical scholarship.

Already in Aristotle the third attitude may be seen. He was far
too good an observer to miss the particularity of the individual,
whether it was a political institution which worked although it did
not fit into his ideal scheme, or a unique phenomenon in nature.
The emphasis thereafter shifts not only in Theophrastus' botany
but also in literature and art from the general to the particular,
from the typical to the individual. Thus the Hellenistic portrait no
longer points the contrast between appearance and reality nor
idealises in an attempt to represent the reality, but shows the

[1] Pl. 12.   [2] Pl. 10a.

reality through the appearance—Theophrastus' Characters are displayed in the details of their dress, conversation, and behaviour; the sculptured portrait shows the orator as he makes his speech, the philosopher giving his lecture, and the poet writing his play. Hellenistic biography seizes on the events and appearances which distinguish its subjects from every one else, and though Menander's characters fall into well-defined types we remember them rather as individual variations on those types. Probably for the first time in the history of drama even their language is individualised.

Each attitude has its own danger: the danger of the first is that one term of the contrast will be unduly depressed by the elevation of the other. The danger of the second is that the organic structure may be used wholly in the service of emotion, and the danger of the third is that the structure may break up altogether. But if we say that Plato overemphasised his Forms and gave them a reality which they did not possess, yet we must also remember that they were a necessary stage in the development to Aristotelian logic and that the first steps were taken by Plato himself in the *Sophist*. And if now we are becoming frightened of the wholesale application of the pattern of organic growth to art, literature, and institutions, we must also remember that we probably owe our knowledge of the ancient Greek world to Aristotle's choice of this simple scheme for collecting knowledge. If we deplore the unscrupulousness of Hellenistic biographers and the intellectual backslidings of the Stoics, we must also remember the sensitiveness of Theophrastus' botany and the discerning sympathy of Menander.

The achievement of the fourth century is after all astonishing if we consider only its most obvious products—the sculpture of Praxiteles and Lysippus, the painting of Pamphilus and Apelles, the prose of Isocrates and Demosthenes, the educational theory of Plato, the logic, scholarship, and science of Aristotle, and New Comedy. According to our own inclinations we may rate one or other achievement higher—the beauty of a marble head or a bronze mirror, of the *Symposium* or the *Epitrepontes*, the idealism of Demosthenes' political speeches, the range and power of Aristotle's thought, or the sympathy with the individual and particular which we see in Lysias' narratives, in Plato's young men, or in Menander's heroines, and which is differently formulated in Aristotle's concept of *epieikeia* and Theophrastus' concept of *oikeiotes*. Athens was a small city and the Greek world was closely interconnected. Together poet and artist, orator and thinker elaborated a conception of human life which could be passed on to the Hellenistic world and Rome and so ultimately to us.

INDEX

(Principal references in Italics)

PLATES

PLATE I

Attic grave-relief of comic poet with two comic masks, ca. 380 B.C.
(cf. pp. 17 ff., 25, 27, 33, 88, 90, 151)

PLATE 2

Attic oenochoe, late fifth century. Smith on holiday
(cf. pp. 18, 148)

PLATE 3

a. Gnathia (Tarentine) fragments, ca. 350/40 B.C.
Tragic actor (cf. p. 19)

b. Attic volute-krater, ca. 400 B.C. Satyr-play
(Pronomos flute-player) (cf. pp. 13, 32, 148)

PLATE 4

a. Attic bell-krater, ca. 370/60 B.C. Heracles
in a chariot (cf. pp. 34, 148)

b. Attic kalyx-krater, Kadmos painter, end of fifth
century. Judgment of Paris (cf. pp. 13, 37, 148, 151)

PLATE 5

a. Attic oenochoe, late fifth century. Heracles
in Centaur chariot (cf. pp. 34, 148)

b. Attic kalyx-krater, Pl. 4*b*, another view

PLATE 6

Marble head of Dionysus by Praxiteles (original or
very good copy) (cf. pp. 39, 150)

PLATE 7

Attic pelike, Meidias painter, late fifth century. Heracles
and Deianira (cf. pp. 13, 39, 42, 81, 148)

PLATE 8

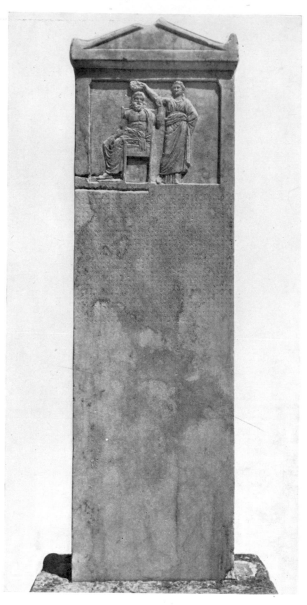

Attic documentary relief, 336 B.C. Democracy
crowns Demos (cf. p. 49)

PLATE 9

Apulian red-figure volute-krater, 330/20 B.C.
Achilles and Thersites (cf. pp. 67, 83, 102)

PLATE 10

a. Attic bell-krater, 360/50 B.C. Initiation of Heracles
and Dioscuri (cf. pp. 79, 84, 148, 152)

b. Attic hydria, 360/50 B.C. Heracles in the garden
of the Hesperides (cf. pp. 81, 148)

PLATE II

Attic pelike, 370/60 B.C. Hunt of the Calydonian boar
(cf. pp. 81, 148)

PLATE 12

Alexander mosaic, copy of original painting ca. 330/20 B.C. (cf. pp. 82 f., 89, 153)

PLATE 13

b. Corinthian bronze mirror, 350/40 B.C.
Nymph bathing in cave (cf. p. 84)

a. Relief from Corinthian bronze hydria, 360/50 B.C.
Eros and Psyche (cf. p. 104)

PLATE 14

Head of Aristotle, copy of original 340/20 B.C. (cf. p. 90)

PLATE 15

Attic relief, ca. 350/40 B.C. Dedication by Olympiodoros, Aristomache, and Theoris to Zeus Epiteleios Philios, his mother Philia, and his wife Agathe Tyche (cf. pp. 7, 103)

PLATE 16

Attic oenochoe, 350/40 B.C. Eros, Pompe, and Dionysus
(cf. pp. 7, 105)